Turning the Tables on
Challenging Behaviour

Turning the Tables on Challenging Behaviour

A practitioner's perspective to transforming challenging behaviours in children,

young people and adults with SLD, PMLD or ASD

Peter Imray

Routledge
Taylor & Francis Group

LONDON AND NEW YORK

First published 2008 by Routledge
2 Park Square, Milton Park, Abingdon, Oxon, OX14 4RN

Simultaneously published in the USA and Canada
by Routledge
280 Madison Ave, New York, NY 10016

Routledge is an imprint of the Taylor & Francis Group, an informa business

Typeset in Celeste and Bliss by RefineCatch Limited, Bungay, Suffolk
Printed and bound in Great Britain by Bell & Bain Ltd, Glasgow

British Library Cataloguing in Publication Data
A catalogue record for this book is available from the British Library

Library of Congress Cataloging in Publication Data
A catalog record for this book has been requested

ISBN 10: 0–415–43758–X (pbk)
ISBN 13: 978–0–415–43758–5 (pbk)

This book is dedicated to my children Dan and Natalie (now very grown up) to whom I owe considerable thanks for not displaying anywhere near the level of challenging behaviour they should have done, given my lack of parenting skills!

Contents

Acknowledgements

I would like to particularly thank the following for their help in realising this book, and apologise to those I've missed out.

To Pam for being so understanding with the time I've stolen to write the book.

To Ed Ashcroft, Ros Blackburn, Caroline Goff, Sally Paveley, Bozena Marczyk and Simon Eccles for their considerable help in the autism sections.

To Mandy Hadfield who's carried me when I should have been working and to Rod Lupton for the title.

To all the staff at The Bridge School for being so supportive and such brilliant practitioners in the realisation of positive behavioural support.

Abbreviations

ABA	Applied Behavioural Analysis
ADHD	Attention Deficit Hyperactivity Disorder
ASD	Autistic Spectrum Disorders
BILD	British Institute of Learning Difficulties
BMP	Behaviour Management Programme
DSI	Dysfunction in Sensory Integration
ESBD	Emotional, Social and Behavioural Difficulties
ILEA	Inner London Education Authority
INSET	In-Service Training
LEA	Local Education Authority
MLD	Moderate Learning Difficulties
NAS	National Autistic Society
PDA	Pathological Demand Avoidance
PECS	Picture Exchange Communication System
PMLD	Profound and Multiple Learning Difficulties
QCA	Qualifications and Curriculum Authority
SALT	Speech and Language Therapist
SEN	Special Educational Need
SI	Sensory Integration
SIB	Self-injurious Behaviours
SLD	Severe Learning Difficulties
TA	Teaching Assistant
TEACCH	Treatment and Education of Autistic and related Communication-handicapped CHildren

Introduction

This is a book about challenging behaviour, but it is also a book about children, young people and adults with severe learning difficulties (SLD) and profound and multiple learning difficulties (PMLD) and to a lesser degree – but only because there is so much published material available – autistic spectrum disorders (ASD). The arguments that run throughout the book are threefold.

Firstly, that there are fundamental principles applying to challenging behaviour ('The Magnificent Seven' as outlined in Chapter 4) which **must** be observed if you are serious about tackling the behaviours and discovering lasting resolutions.

Secondly, effectively tackling a behaviour which challenges demands an identification of the degree of learning difficulty, and the resolution to the problems of the challenging behaviour will vary depending on the nature of that learning difficulty. That is, whilst the same behaviour (whether that be hitting, pinching, scratching, head banging or whatever) may be adopted by an SLD child, a PMLD child or an ASD child, the same strategy **cannot** be applied with an equal expectation of success, but will very much depend upon the degree and type of the learning difficulty. Fundamental to the success of any strategy is the correct identification of the **main** area of learning difficulty and the book is therefore divided into the three main areas of SLD, PMLD and ASD. The ASD section largely concentrates on those who have a dual diagnosis of ASD and SLD, but where the ASD is considered to be the primary area of educational need.

Thirdly, changing behaviour is not just about the child changing – it is very much about **us** changing. There is **no such thing** as behaviour without a reason (**all** behaviours have a reason behind them) and that reason **always** has a meaning. We cannot hope to change the behaviour unless we're prepared to both try and understand **and try to accept** the meaning behind it. At the most basic level challenging behaviours are all communications – they might be poor communications, they might be appalling communications, but they are communications nonetheless and probably the best the child can do. The fact that the behaviour continues usually means that **we have failed** to teach a better way of communicating. This book is about trying to find a better way to teach.

I have very much wanted to make this book a practical guide to challenging behaviour and to this end I have tried to include as many actual case studies as I can. All of these case studies are real, and all of the children and young people are personally known to me, the vast majority having attended The Bridge School at some stage over the last ten years or so, though I have changed their names to protect their privacy. These are however only a small sample of the myriad problems that any teacher, teaching assistant (TA), parent, care worker, therapist, social worker, etc. might encounter at any one particular time. It is not possible to present a definitive guide to every problem that might arise and this book makes no attempt to do so. It does, however, make every effort to outline a set of guiding principles which have a strong base in both theory and practice. It is your task to be flexible enough to utilise these principles so that they can best meet the needs of each individual case of challenging behaviour, and I hope that this book can go some way towards giving you the tools towards achieving that aim. There is, however, no substitute for experience. As part of the research for this book I have had occasion to review the behaviour management programmes I have written over the last ten years or so and have cringed at how awful some of the early ones (and some of the not so early ones!) are. None of us is perfect, and none of us – however expert we claim to be – has the definitive answer. Each child is an individual and each case will have to be treated individually, but the principles apply nonetheless.

Finally, before you enter into the main body of the book, I make no excuses for repeating myself. Anyone who teaches or has dealings with learning difficulties knows the value of repetition in the learning process and if in the process of reading this book you get the feeling that you've read that bit before . . . you probably have!

What is challenging behaviour?

A little while ago I went to a mainstream primary school to deliver after-school INSET (in-service training) on Team-Teach – a whole-setting holistic training approach to behaviour supports and interventions – or in other words restraint and physical handling training. In order to establish which techniques to teach and what areas of training to concentrate on, I asked the staff what sort of problems they experienced with their children.

> *'Well,'* said one teacher, *'some children can be very aggressive.'*
>
> *'What do you mean by aggressive?'* I replied. *'What sort of things do they do?'*
>
> *'Some pupils can be very rude and will occasionally swear at you. I had a boy walk out of class last week without so much as a by-your-leave.'*

Those who are familiar with the daily traumas in the typical SLD class will understand that this reply caused some raised eyebrows amongst my colleagues to the effect that if this was the worst that could happen, what the heck were we doing there in the first place! That would, however, be undermining the real fear and sense of despair that can be engendered by an aggressive, out-of-control 10-year-old who has 'lost the plot' and is directing his anger at you personally. One of the good things about facing challenging behaviour in an SLD setting – if there can be good things about challenging behaviour – is the fact that aggression is rarely personal; you just happen to be in the wrong place at the wrong time.

Nonetheless, the regular occurrences in an SLD school tend to be more varied than that displayed in this mainstream primary school at least. The list below is not exhaustive, but gives a flavour.

- Physical attacks on others, including hitting, kicking, scratching, biting, pinching, pulling hair.
- Spitting, vomiting (projectile and otherwise), regurgitating.
- Deliberate incontinence, soiling, smearing.
- Deliberate fitting.
- Self-injurious behaviours (SIB) including hand and arm biting, head banging, eye gouging, lip biting, skin picking, pulling hair out.
- Shouting, swearing, screaming, making loud noises.
- Pica – the obsessional need to have (non-edible) objects in the mouth.
- Distractibility and hyperactivity.

- Obsessional behaviours.
- Non-compliance and resistance to change.
- Verbal abuse.
- Interfering with or destroying others' work.
- Lack of awareness of danger.
- Inappropriate sexualised behaviour including open masturbation, open touching of others' and their own private parts.
- Running away.
- Dropping to the floor as a dead weight.
- Climbing.
- Throwing.

Clearly some of these are harder to deal with than others, though it is not uncommon in extreme cases for one individual to display many of these behaviours at the same time.

The fact that these behaviours are occurring does not, however, mean that they are challenging *per se*. Climbing, throwing, running and dropping to the floor may be perfectly acceptable in PE or Dance; spitting may be OK when done into a spittoon; head banging may be tolerated in a soft play area. It needs more than just the existence of the behaviours to make them challenging.

Emerson (1995) has defined challenging behaviour as:

> *culturally abnormal behaviour(s) of such an intensity, frequency or duration that the physical safety of the person or others is likely to be placed in serious jeopardy, or behaviour which is likely to seriously limit the use of, or result in the person being denied access to, ordinary community facilities.*

(p. 3)

Zarkowska and Clements (1994) have noted that challenging behaviour:

> *can be acknowledged to exist if it satisfies at least some of the following criteria:*
>
> - *The behaviour itself or its severity is inappropriate given a person's age and level of development.*
> - *The behaviour is dangerous either to the person or to others.*
> - *The behaviour is contrary to social norms.*
> - *The behaviour constitutes a significant additional handicap for the person by interfering with the learning of new skills or by excluding the person from important learning opportunities.*
> - *The behaviour causes significant stress to the lives of those who live and work with the person and impairs the quality of their lives to an unreasonable degree.*

(pp. 2–3)

O'Brien (1998) has stated that:

> *When formulating a school-based definition, the following might be considered:*
>
> - *The behaviour prevents the child from participating in the curriculum.*
> - *The behaviour has a detrimental effect on the learning of other children.*

- *The behaviour is not considered appropriate to the child's age and level of development.*
- *The behaviour results in the child being continually isolated from their peers.*
- *The behaviour has a negative impact upon the child's independence.*
- *The behaviour is placing extreme threats or demands on individual staff, staff teams or school resources.*
- *The behaviour causes the child to be disliked by a significant adult who regularly works with them.*
- *The behaviour reinforces the child's negative self-concept and low self-esteem.*
- *The behaviour is restricting the opportunities for a child to develop new skills.*
- *The behaviour is creating a dangerous environment for the child, for other children and for adults. This would include self-injurious behaviour.*
- *The behaviour has a damaging effect on relationships between the school and the person or persons who have parental responsibility for the child.*

(pp. 71–2)

Behaviour and learning

Both O'Brien (1998) and Harris *et al.* (1993) emphasise the fact that we cannot separate behaviour from learning, indeed Harris goes further in opining that:

> *In describing behaviours as **challenging**, we are acknowledging the interactive relationship between behaviours and the situation in which they occur; we recognise that difficult or troublesome behaviours are a shared responsibility because they **challenge** us to find positive ways of responding.*

(Harris *et al.* 1993, p. 180, original emphasis)

Three issues arise out of this statement, all of them relating to our attitude as managers, teachers, TAs, service providers, parents and carers not only to the children, young people and adults with learning difficulties who might display challenging behaviours but also to the challenging behaviours themselves.

'Getting in the firing line'

In my role as a teacher responsible for managing challenging behaviour and head of a school site which has housed a number of students with severe challenging behaviour over the years, I am often in the position of trying to encourage staff to put themselves 'in the firing line'; that is, to work with pupils who are very likely to hurt them. I am fortunate enough to have had the privilege of working directly with some truly fantastic staff in my time, who not only get into the firing line again and again and again, but generally (especially support staff) get paid a pittance for doing it! They give of themselves day after day, and they do it with love. It is an issue much discussed by Tim O'Brien in his excellent book *Promoting Positive Behaviour* (1998), and it is an issue I will return to again.

There are, however, a few staff who are reluctant travellers, and who disclaim responsibility, saying something like:

> *I do not come to work to get hurt. It is not my job, and I don't get paid enough to deal with severe challenging behaviour which may, after all, cause me stress, anxiety and injury.*

Well, at the risk of upsetting everybody I have two comments to make. **To the persons themselves – you're in the wrong job!** There are lots of jobs that do not involve the risk of physical injury – as far as I know, check-out tills and telephones don't bite. Staying in an SLD school when you don't want to work with challenging behaviours is like working as a nurse when you can't stand needles. Of course, schools must do their utmost to ensure that incidents resulting in injury, however slight, are kept to a minimum, but it is folly to believe that even the best run schools are risk free. Life's too short – do something else!

Secondly, **to the employers of the care assistants, learning support assistants (LSAs) and TAs working in SLD schools – pay your people more!** If you're serious about wanting to improve the quality of your education and care, and I'm assuming you are serious otherwise you wouldn't be reading this book, you have to recognise that the very best resource is your staff. Whatever the case for raising teachers' pay, it pales into insignificance when compared to the injustices that are heaped upon TAs. I have seen many changes to the role of the TA and a steady and inexorable march towards increases in responsibility and the beginnings of a career structure. But a career structure is useless if the pay remains at the lowest levels and whilst schools should certainly be putting pressure on local education authorities (LEAs) (and LEAs on central government) it is not acceptable to merely blame central government. Schools have to start the process themselves. **Schools have to look at their budgets, make savings where they can and transfer those savings to TAs' pay. It can be done and it should be done**.

Getting the right funding and placement

There is another tack that I've also heard a few times, which relates to reaching the breakdown stage, where schools feel they can no longer cope with extremes of behaviour from a particular child or student.

> It is not fair to other (pupils/service users) that they are expected to put up with others' challenging behaviours with all the consequent drain in resources this involves. Pupils with severe challenging behaviour should be separately educated.

Though I have more sympathy with this line since there are undoubtedly going to be persons with extremes of behaviour that even the most clued-up SLD school is not going to be able to manage, not to mention the difficulties parents face at home leading to pressure for a residential placement being applied, it strikes me that schools often miss a trick here in looking for the residential specialist option too early. The ideal option must be that day SLD schools continue to cater for extreme cases, **provided** they are given the resources to do so by the LEA. The table below gives approximate education costings (as at 2007) for each category of child, without any additional allocated staffing unless stated.

On the figures below, it doesn't take a great deal of imagination to work out that it is undoubtedly in the LEA's best interests to keep learners in their local SLD school. Residential placements (assuming of course that one can be found!), especially when behavioural difficulties are involved, are incredibly expensive. Funding for such placements doesn't always fall solely on the LEA, however, and the cost will often be divided between the area health authority, social services

Table 1.1 Approximate 2007 education costings for each category of child

Type of educational provision	Approximate annual cost to the LEA
	£
Mainstream primary	3,000
Mainstream secondary	5,000
SLD placement in special school	10,000
PMLD placement in special school	15,000
SLD placement in residential setting	40,000 plus
SLD placement in a residential setting for behaviour difficulties	75,000 plus
SLD placement in a residential setting for behaviour difficulties with 1 to 1 support	100,000 plus
SLD placement in a residential setting for behaviour difficulties with 24-hour 1 to 1 support	200,000 plus

and education. Nonetheless, any residential placement is still going to represent a sizeable chunk of the total LEA budget.

As long as the major reasons cited for sending learners to residential placements are (i) the difficulties of home life where parents have limited support and (ii) the difficulties of school life where schools have insufficient resources – **it must be in all the funding parties' best interests to plough monies into a school willing to have a real go at resolving behavioural difficulties.** This is especially so when schools can alter behaviours to such a degree that it has a real positive effect upon home life.

What, then, is stopping schools dealing effectively with challenging behaviour? Harris *et al.* (2001) have identified some issues:

- No-one has taken the initiative in dealing with the behaviour.
- A programme is in place, but it is not being managed properly.
- A programme is in place, but there is no sign of it being successful.
- Some staff argue that the behaviour is the person's choice and they shouldn't interfere with it.
- Expert advice is needed but has not been provided.

To these we might also add:

- People are frightened of the behaviour(s) or of the child.
- Some people deal with it in certain ways that others can't.
- Everyone has different, personalised strategies.
- Dealing effectively with the behaviour involves a level of staffing which the organisation does not have.

Forget the curriculum?

Finally, we also need to accept **the primacy of challenging behaviour over and above our concerns with the curriculum**. Whilst severe challenging behaviours occur there is usually very little academic work taking place since all efforts are going towards resolving and minimising the difficulties of the behaviour(s). Nonetheless, we in education are driven by the pretence that academic learning has preference. The Government tells Ofsted; Ofsted tells the LEA; the LEA tells the Headteacher; the Headteacher tells the Deputy Headteacher; the Deputy Headteacher tells the teachers; the teachers tell the TAs; the TAs tell the children with challenging behaviours; the children with challenging behaviours kick, scream, bite, pull hair, wreck work and, worst of all, don't seem to pay the slightest bit of notice to the Government's dictats!

The facts are that for some children – those with severe and habitual challenging behaviours – **learning is learning to deal with their behaviour and absolutely nothing else**. When this is resolved, other types of learning can take place, but not until.

These then are the issues which we need to address and which will be tackled over the rest of the book.

Summary

This chapter has dealt with the sorts of behaviour which those working and living with people who have SLD and PMLD and who display challenging behaviours are likely to deal with on a regular basis. It has also looked to bring out various definitions of challenging behaviour, the most extensive of which is probably Tim O'Brien's (O'Brien 1998), though others are equally valid.

Whatever the definition, the problems can be severe, and carry major consequences for the person with the challenging behaviours, their parents and family, the school or residential placement and, indeed, for society in general.

Challenging behaviours do not, however, happen in an empty room, and we are therefore as much responsible for the challenging behaviour as the person themselves. We need to look at challenging behaviour as a subject to be taught, just as Maths, English or Science is a subject to be taught. In fact, when the challenging behaviour prevents normal learning it becomes **the** subject to be taught, since nothing else can progress until the issues are dealt with.

The challenge to change is not only the learner's, it's also **ours,** and the first **positive** response is, therefore, to celebrate our fantastically privileged position of being able to effect a **real** change and make a **real** difference to a number of lives.

CHAPTER 2

What are severe learning difficulties (SLD) and profound and multiple learning difficulties (PMLD)?

Definitions

Since being involved in starting up The Bridge Professional Training Centre (part of The Bridge School, an all-age SLD/PMLD/ASD school in Islington) in 1997, I have been exercised by the problem of satisfactorily defining the terms 'severe learning difficulties' and 'profound and multiple learning difficulties' to those I train. The thoughts outlined in this chapter are a reworking of those first propounded in *The SLD Experience* (Imray 2005).

There are a number of practitioners who consciously shy away from defining the terms of 'severe learning difficulties' and 'profound and multiple learning difficulties' on the grounds that they unnecessarily pigeonhole, and are therefore likely to limit the potential of the person with learning difficulties. Learning and growth, they argue, take place over the whole of a lifetime and to define a person as being of a particular mental age will inevitably limit the individual to a second-class education. We do not spend our lives insisting upon treating each child as a unique individual (they continue) in order to see them restricted by a label.

This argument might carry weight if the UK education system still discriminated against educating those with learning difficulties, but this is very much not the case. Say what you will about mainstream education, the UK's commitment to special educational need (SEN) provision is comparable to any other country in the world and something of which we should be rightly proud. I do not wish to be complacent in this; we are in the infancy of SLD/PMLD research and education – there is still much to do and many horizons to explore – but the chances of a child being 'locked in' and never fully discovered, as for example with Christy Brown of *My Left Foot* fame (Brown 1954), are thankfully, in the UK at least, now very remote.

One might expect that academics would have more of a stab at the problem, but here it may be that they (in a way rightly) assume that the problem is just too complex. A number of writers (Kiernan 1985, Kangas and Lloyd 1988, Goldbart 1994 and Ouvrey 1998 among others) have noted the dangers of likening conventionally developing children to those with disabilities and it may be that these dangers have proved too much of a barrier to a definition which has both a simple and common meaning. This does not mean, however, that the simple and common are worthless. Many who work in the fields of SLD and PMLD – parents, TAs, care staff, transport staff, teachers new to SEN, associated professionals such as social workers, medical staff, respite workers (the list is very long) – might only have limited interest in exploring a fully detailed academic definition which might satisfy the 'expert'. The definition of a giraffe as a tall animal with four legs and a very long neck might be far too simplistic and general for the zoologist, but it suffices for the casual visitor to the safari park to initially identify the animal.

The reluctance to succinctly define SLD and PMLD has, however, merely resulted in a tendency to rely on experience and an unspoken, shared understanding – or in Richard Aird's words, the ability to 'get a feel for the kind of SEN provision that the pupil might require' (Aird 2001, p. 16). But this, precisely because it is so subjective, will inevitably lead to differing interpretations and much confusion. A definition should be able to give us a clear mental picture and should be understood within a common meaning. It does not imply, however, that it must be either definitive or restricting. A 'copse' creates a different mental picture from a 'wood' which creates a different mental picture from a 'forest'. Although all three have much in common, each word carries a great deal of additional, commonly understood meaning in terms of the surrounding countryside, and the flora and fauna likely to be held within each. Further, each word can be expanded upon and more closely defined if necessary, so that small, large, hillside, tropical, deciduous, coniferous, etc. can, by simple extension, lead to much greater, and indeed clearer, shared understanding.

There is no reason why the same cannot be applied to 'learning difficulty', so that all those involved can share a **common basic understanding**, which can be varied according to the strengths, needs and circumstances of the particular individual.

The standard, IQ-related definition (Grossman *et al.* 1983, Luckasson *et al.* 1992) is fraught with difficulties. Even if IQ tests do measure intelligence – and that is a fairly big if – the level at which they pick up someone with SLD, and especially PMLD, is both arbitrary and totally lacking in shared meaning. Emerson (2001), for example, defines severe intellectual disability as relating to those who 'score below 50 on standardized tests of intelligence' (p. 2), but what meaning exactly does 'below 50' have for you? Whilst possibly useful for the trained psychologist, it is not at all helpful for educators, carers or parents. Other definitions which seek to find a formula for mental age by a mathematical equation which divides chronological age by IQ (Hogg and Sebba 1986) logically leave us with the premise that the longer someone with PMLD lives – and nowadays, that can be well into their twenties and possibly thirties – the less PMLD they actually become.

Ware (2003) makes a more pragmatic attempt to define PMLD by putting a developmental age ceiling of two years. This refers back to the Piaget's (1953) Sensorimotor Period – his first stage of child development – by the end of which the child will be expected to have (i) object permanence (ii) contingency awareness (cause and effect) (iii) the ability to imitate and (iv) moved away from the profound egocentrism that typifies babies, into an understanding that we are all separate individuals with our own thoughts, feelings and lives. It may be, however, that both Piaget and Ware are being overly cautious. Work done by Uzgiris and Hunt (1975) and Dunst (1980) in breaking down the Sensorimotor Period, clearly indicates that the skills outlined above are in place well before 18 months for the conventionally developing child, and it only needs us to think of conversations with the average 2-year-old to recognise that they are very capable individuals who have intellectual, concentration and communicative skills well beyond that which we would normally associate with PMLD.

I would therefore argue that the term PMLD generally defines **any person whose intellectual development is equivalent to a conventionally developing child of under 18 months (and usually considerably under 18 months) irrespective of their actual chronological age.**

This definition does, however, need to be supplemented by noting a number of defining characteristics. Namely, that this population will largely:

- **be pre-verbal in terms of intent**. Where communications initiated by the learner will be proto-imperative (primarily based on needs and wants), rather than the more sophisticated proto-declarative communications used by learners with SLD (Bates *et al.* 1975, Park 1998).

- **have no formal means of communication**. That is, communications will be 'interpreted' by known adults from physical gestures or vocal utterances.

- **be unable to independently imitate** actions, sounds and movements.

- **be totally physically reliant on others** for all their basic care and safety.

- **have numerous sensory difficulties.** These are largely based around their developmental inabilities to integrate sensory stimulation and concentrate down a single sensory channel.

- **be totally unable to conceptualise abstract concepts.** I will elaborate on this more when discussing SLD.

- **have limited contingency awareness and an unrefined sense of cause and effect.** Many learners with PMLD may well be able to press a switch, but very few will have a refined sense of what they are specifically pressing the switch for or, indeed, how to control that supply.

Further riders can be added, in that:

- generally speaking the greater the degree of intellectual impairment, the higher the chance of attendant (multiple) physical impairments;

- the numbers of PMLD are undoubtedly rising (Male 1996);

- the physical disabilities themselves are getting far more complex (Male 1996).

With SLD there seems to be even less consensus, other than the standard (and I would say unhelpful) IQ definitions noted above, but it seems to me that we can utilise the ceiling of our PMLD definition to form a base line, and the expectations of the National Curriculum Level 1 to form an upper level.

Many of the early arguments against the National Curriculum rightly pointed out that the ubiquitous 'W' of Working towards Level 1 gave no indication of how the learner with learning difficulties might be progressing, hence the introduction of P Scales. The National Curriculum indicates that Level 2 should be 'averagely' achieved by the age of seven in mainstream education, but clearly this is likely to be well beyond the vast majority of pupils defined as having SLD. Further, achievement, even within the P Scales, is likely to be fractured and uneven both across different subject areas and within each subject area, a fact which has been recognised by the Qualifications and Curriculum Authority's (QCA's) espousal of the 'best fit' scenario (QCA 2001). This in turn implies that (for a multitude of reasons) academic achievement will be much harder to both realise and maintain for the SLD pupil.

Latham and Miles (2002) indicate that the communication skills required to achieve P7 and P8 are evident in conventionally developing children at between three and five years of age, but are of sufficient sophistication to require them to do such things as: understand and express reasons and predictions; plan activities; negotiate; question to find out information; understand abstract ideas and language out of context (e.g. jokes); and use complex sentences containing joining words such as 'and', 'because', etc.

Similarly both Gibson (1989) and Grove (1998) posit that conventionally developing children achieve fluency in reading from the age of five onwards and are able to deal with print in a number of ways; that is, understand the rules and subtleties of language such as affixes, suffixes, analogy, etc. and process print details (understand what they are reading) automatically.

Extending the thought posed within the PMLD definition, it only needs us to think of the abilities demonstrated by the 'average' 6-year-old to realise that this level of attainment would represent a real high-flier within the vast majority of SLD schools in the UK.

Grasping the nettle again, therefore, I would define someone with SLD as being **any person whose developmental age is equivalent to a conventionally developing child of under six (and usually considerably under six) irrespective of their chronological actual age.**

Once again, there are clear defining characteristics.

- **Communication difficulties**. These may vary from having only a limited formal communication system to having a reduced or restricted receptive and/or expressive vocabulary. The key area of difference with PMLD is, however, that SLD communicators have the motivation, ability and persistence to use proto-declarative communications, that is, regard communication as an end in itself and be able to initiate such communications.

- **Difficulties with abstract concepts**. The most obvious area affected being mathematical understanding, with concepts such as conservation, general use of number, 'nothing' as a number, time, money, etc. being obvious areas that SLD pupils find problematic. Staves (2001) points out that 'social maths' as opposed to 'personal maths' comes with the development of cognitive and communication skills in order to describe quantities, space, time and change, and normally requires an understanding of numbers above two. Other significant areas also affected are an incomplete and often inadequate understanding of time and a deficit in the ability to understand emotions and feelings, especially their own.

- **Difficulties in moving things from the short- to the long-term memory**. It still puzzles me that the typical SLD pupil will invariably remember the most intimate details of friends they haven't seen for several years, yet not be able to remember what they did 5 minutes ago, or which bus they get on at the end of the day, even though it's been parked in the same spot at 3.30 p.m. for the last 5 years! Much research still needs to be done in this area.

- **Difficulties in maintaining concentration**. This is clearly very strongly related to both memory and the ability to ignore non-essential sensory stimuli, such as the school bus driving past the window!

- **General (child-like) innocence**. This particularly differentiates the SLD pupil from the 'street-wise' moderate learning difficulties (MLD) and emotional, social and behavioural difficulties (ESBD) pupils.

How do these definitions affect our responses to challenging behaviour?

Cause and effect

A fundamental difference between the two learning categories is the relative contingency awareness within each group, or in other words, their respective understanding of cause and effect. It is evident that persons with profound learning difficulties have no clear understanding that their actions affect those around them. It is clear that the profound egocentrism (Piaget 1953) which affects small babies – where they believe that the whole world centres around them – does not allow them an understanding of how others feel about the behaviour. If I slapped my headteacher round the face I would have a fair idea of the consequences – the sack springs to mind! – but there is no reason to believe that someone with PMLD would either be aware of, or care about, the consequences. Those with SLD, on the other hand, have a much stronger and better developed understanding of cause and effect.

Communicative opportunities

Given the level of difficulty that most people with learning difficulties have in communicating and gaining even their basic needs, never mind more complicated issues like emotional state, it is a source of constant amazement to me that there are a large number of people with SLD or PMLD who **do not** have significant challenging behaviours. Clearly, the more severe the communication difficulties, the more likely it is that opportunities to express needs and preferences will be limited. This in turn, can only increase the likelihood of significant challenging behaviour.

The level of learning difficulty

This is likely to significantly affect an individual's ability to reflect on their own behaviour and understand their own feelings and emotions. There is likely to be considerably less natural empathy for others' feelings and emotions (a state also common in ASD) which makes appeals to those with PMLD to 'be nice' or 'be good' meaningless. Unfortunately also, the more common instructions given to those with PMLD (and ASD) like '**Don't do that** because you're hurting me' or '**Don't do that** because others don't like it' are equally negative and pointless. They might make you feel better, but they will do nothing to change the behaviour and are actually likely to be counterproductive in the longer term.

Summary

A central theme of this book is that we have to know the person we are dealing with before we can even hope to tackle the behaviour; the more information we can gain the more chance we have of resolving the problems. Central to this is having a clear understanding of the nature of the person's learning difficulties with a clear and agreed definition of both 'severe learning difficulties' and 'profound and multiple learning difficulties'.

The fundamental difference between the groups is in their ability to understand contingency awareness, or cause and effect. Persons with SLD are (by definition) able to understand that their actions have an effect on others and are therefore open to behaviourist methods of teaching and learning. Those with PMLD do not have a sufficiently refined sense of cause and effect to make behaviourist methods of teaching and learning workable. For those with PMLD, we are into the long haul, where changes in behaviour have to be grounded in the strength and love of our own relationships with them. Lasting changes are equally possible with those with PMLD, it's just that such changes may take months and, quite possibly, years of patient and persistent application to effect.

What is autistic spectrum disorder (ASD)?

If you've just picked this book up casually from the bookshop shelf and have turned to this chapter because you want to find out all about autistic spectrum disorders – stop right here. Put this book back on the shelf and go to the Autism section where there are many hundreds of very learned tomes available. Moving through in degrees of difficulty I might recommend *The Curious Incident of the Dog in the Night-Time* by Mark Haddon (Vintage 2004) – a novel, but an ingeniously constructed one that gives an excellent insight into higher functioning autism (not, note, Asperger's) even if the book itself does not mention autism (or Asperger's) once; *Freaks, Geeks and Asperger Syndrome* by Luke Jackson (Jessica Kingsley 2002) and *Nobody Nowhere* by Donna Williams (Jessica Kingsley 1999) – both being well-written accounts from individuals diagnosed with Asperger Syndrome and autism respectively; and for those seeking a more academic analysis, *Theory of Mind and the Triad of Perspectives on Autism and Asperger Syndrome* by Olga Bogdashina (Jessica Kingsley 2006) is slightly harder to read but well rounded, up to date and full of thought-provoking little asides.

In relation however to ASD and SLD (as a dual diagnosis) I can do no better than to refer you to Rita Jordan, who is probably **the** world authority on ASD/SLD and there is just about everything you need to know in *Autism with Severe Learning Difficulties*. Rita is also, by the way, an excellent speaker (clear, well delivered, with a nice sideline in dry wit) and if you get a chance to hear her – take it.

In lieu of these excellent books, this chapter will attempt to summarise the main defining characteristics of autistic spectrum disorders and address issues around dual diagnosis.

It is vital to state right from the start, however, that as far as behavioural issues are concerned, the vast majority of challenging behaviour problems relating to autism (with or without an additional learning difficulty) can be fairly simply resolved by understanding the nature of the autistic learning style and how very different that can be from more conventional learning styles (see Chapter 7 'Challenging behaviour and autistic spectrum disorders', for a more detailed discussion on this). It is also important to note that we can get blinded by 'autistic behaviours' or at least what are seen as 'autistic behaviours' and there is still much confusion over what constitutes autism – especially in special educational needs, special needs schools and other educational establishments, and how that translates into the educational process.

Defining autistic spectrum disorders

Although both Kanner (1943) and Asperger (1944) noted the existence of autism as a unique developmental disorder hitherto undiagnosed, it wasn't until Wing and Gould (1979) that the concept of a spectrum was discussed – that is, the idea that whilst a number of people may be regarded as autistic, they may be affected to differing degrees, some severe, some much less so, most with learning difficulties, but some without. This work also came up with what still constitutes the basic definition of the Triad of Impairments – Communication, Social interaction, Imagination – and others have put forward what they consider to be common psychological characteristics of autism within the concepts of Theory of Mind and Central Coherence. There is also some brief discussion of sensory issues – what many consider to be the fourth impairment.

The Triad of Impairments

Communication

The child may not develop communication at all, and although they might be able to speak, it does not necessarily mean that they can communicate. Even if they can communicate, they may have a very concrete understanding of language in that 'what you say' is what is understood; as for example in 'Go to the toilet and wash your hands' when what is meant is 'Go and wash your hands in the wash-basin next to the toilet'. No account is taken of nuance, context and alternative (commonly understood) meanings. Even those high-functioning individuals with Asperger's who may develop normal language skills, will not necessarily be able to use it like everyone else – perhaps similar to the condition commonly encountered in SLD schools of learners being able to count without understanding number. The fact that you can talk, read, sign, pass over a symbol, etc. does not automatically mean that you can communicate effectively.

Ros Blackburn, herself autistic and another expert you must hear if you can, has given an example of context during her excellent talk 'Logically Illogical' in reference to an incident when she was booked to give a talk at a particularly large conference. In this context, there are three things you need to know about Ros (i) she has excellent linguistic skills (ii) she always checks where the exits are in unfamiliar venues just in case she has to make a quick getaway and (iii) she doesn't drink coffee because the caffeine is likely to send her 'over the edge'. Upon entering the venue, Ros was directed to an employee of the conference who asked:

'Would you like to sign in?'

'No thank you,' said Ros.

'Well I'm afraid that you have to sign in,' replied the helper, slightly taken aback, 'it's fire regulations you understand'.

'All right,' said Ros and promptly signed in the appropriate place.

Ros was then directed into the main conference area where a waitress approached and said, 'Would you like a cup of coffee?'

At which point Ros fled on the basis that in this place at least 'would you like' meant that she 'had to' and if she **had to** have coffee this was not the place for her!

It should also be noted that people with autism are likely to have problems with all areas of communication regardless of the level of language acquisition, and autism is probably the only disorder where language and communication develop independently of each other. That is, simply because a person can talk (and often talk very eloquently in Ros's case) it does not mean that they can either communicate or understand others' communications, any more than the ability to read means that they have understood what they've read or the ability to count means that they have understood number.

Social interaction

The child with ASD may have difficulty in 'reading the thoughts' and feelings of others, especially in applying flexibility to accommodate changes in social situations. They generally find relationships difficult and indeed extreme forms of autism may see no purpose in relationships that do not benefit them in some measurable way. Christopher Boone (the hero of *The Curious Incident of the Dog in the Night-Time*) has a favourite dream when everybody in the world gets killed by a virus; then

> *I can go anywhere in the world and I know that no one is going to talk to me or touch me or ask me a question. But if I don't want to go anywhere I don't have to, and I can stay at home and eat broccoli and oranges and liquorice laces all the time, or I can play computer games for the whole week, or I can just sit in the corner of the room and rub a pound coin backwards and forwards over the ripple shape on the surface of the radiator.*
>
> (Haddon 2004, p. 242)

Imagination

The child with ASD may appear to be unable to think imaginatively, especially noticeable in role playing and make-believe games. The child may use toys in apparently bizarre ways – lining up toy cars in set orders rather than driving them – and the child may play by engaging in stereotypical behaviours, or at least in ways that ensure that they are in charge of the rules of the game. Games therefore become single-person activities, rather than opportunities to explore relationships and different roles. This deficit – the inability to play imaginatively **with other people** – automatically debars the child from learning about states of mind other than their own and indeed significantly reduces their chances of understanding even their own state of mind. It is also directly related to the lack of Theory of Mind so apparent in those within the autistic spectrum (see below).

Importantly, Rita Jordan (Jordan 2001) argues that the triad should be renamed as:

1 Communication;

2 Social development (rather than 'Social interaction');

3 Flexibility in thinking and behaviour (rather than 'Imagination');

thereby implying that learning – and therefore change – can and does take place. The movement from *Imagination* to *Flexibility* also gives more central recognition to the extreme difficulties autistic people have with change, a matter largely relating to control (see Chapter 4 'The Magnificent Seven' and also dealt with more fully in Chapter 7 'Challenging behaviour and autistic spectrum disorders').

The fourth impairment?

Much discussion has taken place in recent years as to whether **sensory issues** should be classified as the fourth impairment. Certainly, there is considerable evidence to suggest that sensory impairments of one form or another (and often of several forms for the same person!) play a major part in the difficulties faced by people with autism. The issue is further complicated by the fact that there are also two distinct strands of difficulty related to sensory impairment, namely hyper-sensitivity and hypo-sensitivity. Whilst most of those on the spectrum will suffer from **hyper-sensitivity** – being **over-sensitive** or intolerant to an experience – some may suffer from **hypo-sensitivity** – being **under-sensitive** to, or unaware of, an experience. Remember that these sensitivities are not necessarily physical impairments – in that the physical ability to hear, see, touch, taste or smell are impaired – but are more likely to be perceptual impairments, where the message getting to the brain gets jumbled up and confused along the way.

As far as challenging behaviour is concerned, additional complications arise from the fact that people with ASD tend to be extremely sensitive to (often even seemingly slight) changes in the environment and changes in themselves. If the wind gets up, we who do not have autism turn our coat collars up and lean into it; if there's too much noise in the place we're in we either block the noise out or move to another quieter space; if there are flickering lights which upset us, we don't look at them; if we need a drink, we get a drink; if we're hungry, we eat; if we're upset, we seek comfort from others or try to rationalise the feelings. People with autism, however, have considerable difficulty in responding to competing sensory experiences and are often unable to concentrate on more than one thing at a time. For those who are over-sensitive to visual stimulation, asking them to look at you *and* concentrate on what you're saying could easily be one instruction too many.

Although I have tried to offer a rough guide to resolving basic sensory problems in Chapter 7 'Challenging behaviour and autistic spectrum disorders', the whole issue of sensory impairments is dealt with in some depth by (amongst others) Brenda Smith Myles *et al.* (2001) and Olga Bogdashina (2006) and I would refer you to them if you are interested in a more detailed analysis.

Theory of Mind

Numerous writers (Baron-Cohen *et al.* 1985, Camaioni 1992, Bogdashina 2006, for example) have expounded on the fact that those on the autistic spectrum have generally not acquired Theory of Mind. They recognise that it takes some time for conventionally developing children to develop an understanding that they are beings which think and function independently, but most start to achieve this by around 18 months to 2 years and should have a fairly refined sense by 4 years. Initially, as small babies, children are essentially profoundly egocentric; that is, they regard the whole world as being centred on them, all things existing within a kind of bubble with them at the centre. Their mother is in the bubble, milk and food is in the bubble, toys, siblings, significant others, potties, their own toes, the family dog, the local park are all in the bubble. At about 18 months old, however, they will start to have a basic understanding that other people may well have different thoughts and feelings from themselves. By 4 years old the conventionally developing child will demonstrate quite a sophisticated capacity to recognise mental states (intentions, desires, beliefs, etc.) in both themselves and others and be able to use such concepts to explain and predict what they or others might say or do in different social situations. Nobody formally teaches us how to recognise when a person is sad, happy, anxious, stressed, afraid, jealous or angry. Nobody teaches us to recognise and differentiate when a person is slightly anxious, pretty anxious, seriously anxious, majorly anxious, wetting themselves with anxiety or, indeed, pretending to be anxious. We're taught how to always start a sentence with a capital letter; we're taught that the Normans invaded England in 1066; we're taught how to drive a car and how to operate a mobile phone; but nobody teaches us to how to read faces, how to empathise, how to recognise different social situations, how to differentiate sarcasm and irony from gentle teasing. People with autism are as disabled as bats without sonar.

At the risk of sounding like Donald Rumsfeld on a bad day, having a sophisticated Theory of Mind will include an understanding that we all know things that other people don't know and that just because you know something, it doesn't mean that other people know it too. This is best described by the act of lying. People lie because they believe they have information that others don't have and they try to take advantage of that fact, and children learn to lie almost as soon as they start to develop Theory of Mind. A number of us who are parents have been in the situation where a bar of chocolate or some other goodie has gone missing and our little one is vehemently denying all knowledge despite the fact that her face and hands are covered in the stuff! She knew you weren't in the room when she took the chocolate – she knows something you don't know – and because she has Theory of Mind, she knows you don't know she took the chocolate because you were in the garden when she took it! Unfortunately for the little girl, lying is an art that takes some years to master and she still has a long way to go, yet the act of lying clearly indicates that she is not on the spectrum. If she was on the spectrum, she would see absolutely no point in lying since any information she had would automatically be shared by everyone else, including you.

The supposition that people on the autistic spectrum do not have Theory of Mind goes some way to explaining why so many autistic children do not speak anywhere near as early as their conventionally developing peers. We learn to speak in order to socialise, to negate, to exercise choices, to offer and request information, to request assistance and to express feelings, emotions and attitudes. It is after all the best way to communicate; but why communicate at all if everyone knows what you're thinking and why communicate if we all think the same way? Why tell someone you're hungry when they know it already? Why bother to speak when everyone knows what you're thinking, because everyone thinks the same things at the same time? When you couple this with the communicative problems emanating from the Triad, it's no wonder that the motivation to speak is lacking and that speech is often significantly delayed.

Central Coherence

The lack of Central Coherence noted by Frith (1989) is essentially the phenomenon of seeing lots of different and often unrelated pieces rather than the picture as a whole – or in the autistic un-friendly language of the metaphor – the inability to see the wood for the trees. Non-autistic people can generally tell you the plot (or main elements) of a book or a film in a few sentences but autistic people are, in Frith's words, 'detached' from the whole. They will be able to see lots of parts but cannot easily tell which is the most important and you might therefore get a retelling of the whole film, including credits, incidental music, special sound effects and whole chunks of dialogue with the tone of voice and accent faithfully reproduced to fit each character.

The idea of lacking central coherence originally came about to explain the considerable success of autistic people (both with and without additional learning difficulties) in finding hidden angled shapes within a larger meaningful shape – as in Embedded Figures Tests. Here non-autistic people are drawn to seeing the meaningful pram or rocking horse or house, and find it very difficult to detach themselves from the whole picture. Autistics, on the other hand, naturally detach themselves from the whole and therefore pick up each individual shape within it (such as a triangle or an oblong or a cuboid) much more readily. For people with autism the parts become more important than the whole so that some have the ability to make up quite complicated jigsaws without any reference to the picture. For the non-autistic there really is no point to completing a jigsaw without the picture, because it's the picture which holds the meaning.

This ability of the autistic to disregard context is excellent for such tests, but obviously causes considerable problems making sense of ordinary life where the context often gives considerable additional meaning, as noted by Ros Blackburn earlier in this chapter.

Autism and Asperger's

It is estimated that around 80 per cent of people on the autistic spectrum will have an additional learning difficulty which will usually be severe to moderate. Generally, the remaining 20 per cent on the autistic spectrum without an additional learning difficulty are likely to have Asperger Syndrome, though be careful not to generalise around these figures too much because there are still a number of high-functioning people with autism rather than Asperger's, such as Ros Blackburn, Temple Grandin and Donna Williams. Those with Asperger Syndrome will, therefore, suffer equally from the Triad of Impairments and are likely to experience additional, and often severe, sensory difficulties, though they will not have an additional learning difficulty. Apart from this latter point, the **major** difference between the two groups is one of their attitude to relationships. Those with autism and Asperger's can both have extreme and multi-dimensional confusions about relationships, and both are likely to lack the intuitive sense of 'what's going on' which non-autistic people use all the time, but people with Asperger's will generally always desire relationships of one sort or another. For further reading see Marc Segar's *Coping: A Survival Guide for People with Asperger Syndrome*, a particularly well-written, amusing and poignant observation of the difficulties of Asperger's.

Other (apparently) related disorders

There has been, and continues to be, considerable and often very heated debate on what other disorders constitute having a membership within the spectrum (and this includes Asperger Syndrome) but it is not within my remit to concern myself overly with these issues here. Suffice it to say that strategies for dealing with challenging behaviour and ASD as expounded in Chapter 7 'Challenging behaviour and autistic spectrum disorders' can probably be very usefully applied to both Fragile X and attention deficit hyperactivity disorder (ADHD). If, however, you're looking for advice on someone diagnosed with pathological demand avoidance (PDA), a wholly different series of strategies need to be applied and I would refer you to work done by Elizabeth Newson and her colleagues at pdacontact.org.uk where you can download several articles.

Numerous other disorders – depending on who you read – surface every now and then but the only one I'll refer to here is Rett Syndrome. Rett Syndrome is a complex and degenerative neurological disorder which mainly affects girls – there have recently been a few boys diagnosed, though these diagnoses have been very rare. Although present at birth, it only really becomes evident during the second year when 'normal' skills learned start to be lost. Whilst there is variability in the severity of the disorder, the vast majority of people with Rett Syndrome are profoundly and multiply disabled and highly dependent on others for all their needs throughout life. I am somewhat surprised (to say the least) that Rett's figures on the 'autism' list, but take this as indicative of confusions over learning styles that seems to figure quite strongly within the world of SEN.

Autism and severe/profound learning difficulties

The current debate on the incidence of autism seems to indicate that there has been a steady 'rise' over the years. Just to take a few studies of autism (all of which include Asperger's) Wing and Gould (1979) estimated 1 in 250; Ehlers and Gillberg (1993) estimated 1 in 141; and the most recent study in *The Lancet* (Baird *et al.* 2006) estimated 1 in 100. Whilst there are as many numbers as there are studies, the apparent rise has deep significance for all schools, because the learning style and needs of ASD children are so fundamentally different from non-autistic learners.

In 2002, the National Autistic Society (NAS) conducted a survey which estimated the incidence of ASD in the UK at that time as 1 person in every 250 (Barnard *et al.* 2002). The NAS approached a cross-section of schools, and asked senior managers in the schools to estimate the autistic incidence amongst their own pupils, with the following results:

Secondary mainstream pupils	1 in 268
Primary mainstream pupils	1 in 80
All special schools	1 in 3

The secondary response is in accordance with the NAS's own estimation, but the primary response is interesting and seems to indicate a growing recognition of ASDs which previously might have gone undiagnosed. An analogy might be taken by studying crimes of rape over the last 50 years. Certainly the numbers have increased dramatically in this time, but does this mean that there's been an increase in the incidence of rape? Perhaps, but a more likely explanation is an increased awareness of rape as a crime, a resultant increased willingness to report rape, to charge and convict for rape and indeed the significant changes in the definition of rape – the possibility of rape within marriage being taken seriously 50 years ago by anyone apart from the woman being raped, doesn't even bear thinking about!

The special schools figures are however startling! For those of us who have been working in special schools for longer than 10 years or so, we will also wonder where all these autistic children have been hiding, because they certainly weren't apparent to that degree in SLD schools then. Yet the more we look back, the more we might recognise some children who were always regarded as 'strange', 'obsessional', 'obstinate', 'wanting their own way all the time' or who were just downright 'awkward' and virtually all exhibited challenging behaviours; but would these make up the 1 in 3?

Perhaps some small part of the answer lies in the respective definitions. Going back to the last chapter, we ascertained that some of the defining characteristics of severe and profound learning difficulties were:

- communication difficulties;
- difficulties in abstract concepts – for example in understanding emotional states;
- problems with (especially) peer relationships;
- difficulties in concentration;
- difficulties with sensory processing;
- obsessional and stereotypical behaviour;
- difficulties with change and generalisation.

Any of these seem familiar within the general discussion on autism? Couple this with the tendency to define challenging behaviour by the behaviours themselves and it is perhaps not surprising that many within special schools regard a third of their pupils as having autism. Just typing in 'Rett Syndrome' and 'autism' into a search engine brought up a number of organisations that have linked the two.

At the Center for the Study of Autism in Oregon website, Edelson (2006) stated that:

> *children afflicted with Rett Syndrome often exhibit autistic-like behaviors, such as repetitive hand movements, prolonged toe walking, body rocking, and sleep problems.*

Whilst the link between Rett's and autism appears to be a genetic one in that there are biochemical relationships within the MeCP2 gene (Rett Syndrome Research Foundation (Edelson 2006)), it might be **our tendency to confuse the behaviours with the reasons behind the behaviours** (not only in Rett's but in severe/profound learning difficulties generally) that is at fault.

There has undoubtedly been a rise in the number of children with SLD and PMLD diagnosed as autistic, but are these all realistic diagnoses? If not, may a false diagnosis cause confusion? Clearly, this depends on the individual concerned, the degree of the learning difficulty and the degree of the autism. We have to be sure about the autism, but if we are sure, the strategies recommended in Chapter 7 'Challenging behaviour and autistic spectrum disorders' will be relevant.

Secondly, and much more importantly, the concept of inclusion (and inclusion is as powerful a concept in special as in mainstream schools) may have a significant effect on the incidence of behavioural issues where profoundly autistic children are being educated in the same classrooms as those with SLD. Before the 'rise' in incidence of autism, those with what would currently be considered a dual diagnosis were taught without differentiation with their SLD peers, mainly because teachers knew no better; now they're often taught together because to do otherwise is seen as politically incorrect!

The key area to reducing challenging behaviour amongst those with autism is to provide an environment where they can learn free from anxiety, stress and confusion, where the needs of the autism are automatically dealt with and where the individual can concentrate without having to worry about competing sensory demands. People with autism tend not to be able to learn in large groups, they react badly to lots of noise, change and high excitement – they tend to need a calm, ordered, structured environment where routine and certainty are to the fore. Anyone who has observed outstanding teaching in SLD schools, however, will know that people with SLD revel in teaching that is dynamic, innovative, charismatic, energetic, lively and enthusiastic. This is not to say that the best ASD teaching is not energetic and enthusiastic, but that the energy and enthusiasm is largely directed towards ensuring routine and certainty! In the words of Rita Jordan:

> *it is important to recognise that autism leads to a difference in development, not just a delay, and approaches for children with SLD (no matter how effective for children without autism) need to be adapted to take account of that difference.*
>
> (Jordan 2001, p. 16)

I will put it a little stronger in my belief that schools that automatically teach SLD and ASD in the same classrooms (on the grounds of inclusion) are demanding an extraordinarily high level of differentiation from their teachers and TAs – and it may be that these demands are both unreasonable and unattainable.

Summary

Autism is a pervasive neurological disorder that affects all areas of the person's life but is particularly problematic in the areas of communication, social development and flexibility of thought and behaviour. People with autism are particularly challenged in basic social skills, which most non-autistic people take for granted, and tend to find it much easier to deal in detail rather than look at the 'whole picture'. These core features are durable over time, and are accompanied by rituals, compulsions, high levels of anxiety and a desire for sameness.

As far as behavioural issues are concerned, the vast majority of challenging behaviour problems relating to autism (with or without an additional learning difficulty) can only be resolved by understanding the nature of the autistic learning style and adapting **our** behaviour to allow for it. There is little doubt that there has been a significant increase in the dual diagnosis of SLD/ASD over the last few years and this has often placed considerable strain on the resources of SLD schools. It is equally certain however that schools must address the issue of teaching and learning styles and question whether they have found the correct balance between inclusion and teaching according to need.

CHAPTER 4

'The Magnificent Seven'

There are a number of buzzwords involved in challenging behaviour. It is best to make copies of these words and paste them around your room, but make sure that you lock the originals away in a very safe place because if ever you lose them resolving the difficulties might be quite hard, if not impossible, to achieve. These seven ('The **Magnificent** Seven') key words are:

1 **Why?**
2 **Consistency**
3 **Positive**
4 **Reward**
5 **Control**
6 **Time**
7 **Success**

Why?

The reasons for challenging behaviour in people with SLD and PMLD are rich and numerous. There are other writers who have expounded eloquently on this and I would particularly refer you to Hewett (1998b) and Harris *et al.* (2001), though essentially, it doesn't take a great deal of imagination to come up with a few of the more obvious reasons. Some of these might be communication problems; situational fear and uncertainty; dislike of change; an inability to understand emotions, etc., etc. – the list is pretty long. It may be that we can't find out why, as, for example, in the last straw effect, that the cause is hidden within an overwhelming cloud of problems or that there are **lots** of problems all piling in on the person at once.

Not knowing the reason why can cause us a lot of anxiety, especially when we spend so much time and effort trying to be patient and kind and thoughtful, only to get our hair pulled, our ankles kicked or our faces slapped for our troubles. And, of course, not knowing the reason why goes with the territory of SLD and PMLD, since it is likely that the person themselves will be unable to tell us exactly how they are feeling even if they do actually know. Some behaviours are so bizarre that they defy logical explanation, and there is sometimes the additional factor of psychosis to complicate matters even further.

We should, however, make every effort to find out why a particular behaviour occurs and there are several logical courses of action to take.

Parents, carers and family

We were much puzzled by a new student named Ahmed (an SLD student functioning around P4 with a number of autistic-type tendencies) who refused to go to the toilet – or at least he would go, but refused to sit on the toilet or actually urinate in the urinal. On enquiring of his family, we were informed that there were no problems at home, so we assumed he just needed to get used to our environment. Time went on, however, and still he refused, so we instituted a number of behavioural strategies, but without any real success. Further enquiries to his parents, talking specifically about why he wouldn't sit on the toilet, elicited the information that Ahmed was used to having the toilet seat wiped before he sat down from a very young age. We did this, and lo and behold, there were no problems – in that area at least! Asking questions is therefore about **asking the right questions of the right people**.

Other professionals

There is sometimes a tendency amongst class staff (and especially amongst teachers!) to see it as a sign of weakness or professional incompetence if they can't handle challenging behaviours, or are seen to be having problems with particular children or issues. Challenging behaviour is, however, very much a matter of a trouble shared is a trouble halved. Rather than a sign of weakness, opening out the problem to as many people as possible and seeking advice from others is an indication that the organisation is healthy. Individuals too often **pretend** they have the situation under control when all they are doing is fire fighting and trying to avoid major explosions. **Dealing with challenging behaviour is not easy – nobody knows all the answers.**

Observations

It is often really difficult, if not impossible, to see what's causing a behaviour when you are so busy dealing with the consequences of that behaviour. Because children tend not to stand still – especially not those with challenging behaviours – we are so busy mopping up that there is no time or opportunity for reflection. It is vital to take time away from managing in order to just look – it really is quite amazing what you can see. You can use a simple ABC style of observation which notes:

1   A – Antecedent (what happened just before the behaviour);

2   B – Behaviour;

3   C – Consequences (what happened after the behaviour which can sometimes be the 'pay-off' for the child).

Alternatively you can use the slightly more complex STAR chart (Zarkowska and Clements 1994):

1 **S** – Setting (where and when the behaviour occurs);

2 **T** – Triggers (what causes the behaviour);

3 **A** – Action (a description of the behaviour itself);

4 **R** – Result (what happened after the behaviour).

The third option is to merely write down everything you see. If you want to be very scientific you may wish to explore observation techniques further, in which case I would refer you to McBrien and Felce (1992), O'Brien (1998) or Emerson (2001), but generally an ABC or STAR chart suffices. The important things are to give yourself time away from classroom or care involvement (don't try and teach/assist and observe at the same time), conduct at least two or three observations at different times of the day, write up your notes straight away and discuss your findings with your colleagues.

As a general rule with children, young people and adults with SLD or PMLD it is both pointless and negative asking **them** why they committed a particular act. You'd get a shock if one of them said 'Well actually I hit Billy because I've had a very difficult life, what with severe learning difficulties and everything, and I'm seeking more attention from the teacher as a result'. If **you** don't know why, somebody with severe learning difficulties is hardly likely to know, and because of the communication and learning problems, knowing for sure is always a little bit of guesswork.

There is no doubt, however, that finding out why is important, even if it is sometimes extremely difficult to come up with a definitive answer. Fortunately, it is not absolutely essential to know the reason for the behaviour in order to begin dealing with it. It is possible to short-cut the process simply because, to paraphrase Carr and Durand (1985), **all reasons have a tendency to surface as behaviours in one of two broad categories**:

1 Task (or situation) avoidance;

2 Attention seeking.

It should be noted here that I am only referring to SLD and PMLD. With those on the autistic spectrum there could well be many other factors involved which are dealt with in more detail in Chapter 7 'Challenging behaviour and autistic spectrum disorders'.

Since, however, both task (or situation) avoidance and attention seeking are essentially about the learners' attempts to gain **control**, I will discuss them further under that heading.

Consistency

I used to teach that a behaviour policy has very little chance of working if everyone is doing their own thing, but I don't believe that to be true any more. Now I believe that **a behaviour policy has *no* chance of working if everyone is doing their own thing**. Essentially this means that everyone within an organisation who regularly comes into contact with the person – be that at a school, a home, a residential unit, an adult day centre, a respite centre or wherever the person with challenging behaviours might spend time – must follow an agreed policy and work within agreed guidelines if the strategy is to be successful. You may have different strategies within each organisation (that is, home might use a different strategy to school) but you must not have different strategies within the same organisation.

Let's discuss these issues further.

Common ownership of a behaviour management programme

For an individual behaviour policy to be at its best, it has to be 'owned' by all the people it affects. It can only be owned by all the people it affects if they have all had a chance to discuss the issues, air their doubts, put forward their ideas and make clear their points of view. In so many schools that are experiencing difficulties with challenging behaviour, the behaviour management programme is decided by a very small group (the class team), sometimes even just one person (the class teacher), sometimes one person who doesn't even teach the student (the Head or Deputy Head). But I don't know of any schools where the students stay in one class with the same team all the time. There are playtimes and lunchtimes and assembly times and other times when other staff are involved. However good the programme, there is always likely to be one worker (and perhaps more than one) who thinks they know better and will act in a different way as a result. Maybe they actually do know better, but the student will never benefit from this because nobody's listening. If they don't know better – perhaps using fear or bribery to get the student to behave 'just for me' – the student gets mixed messages and will quickly learn to divide and rule. It's what children have always done with parents who don't talk to each other, and it's what children will always continue to do because it can be an effective way of wresting back control from the 'all powerful' adults.

Meetings really *are* important

Managers, therefore, have a very important role to play here, because firstly they have to create the conditions whereby whole-school meetings on challenging behaviour can take place (and that may mean investing resources to pay staff to stay on for after-school meetings) and secondly because they have to chair the meetings so that all have the opportunity to have a say whilst still reaching a decision. That is a particular and precious skill.

It is not necessary for all institutions to follow the same programme

It is generally much harder for parents and families to follow a set programme than it is for other institutions like a school, respite centre or adult training centre. This is because there are generally a limited number of adults (sometimes only one) and dealing with challenging behaviour can be a full-time occupation in itself. Parents will sometimes give in to the demands for a quiet life, simply because it is too exhausting to do otherwise and because there are likely to be other siblings to look after and other demands to be met. Whilst it is undoubtedly the ideal for both home and school to use the same strategies, it is often unreasonable for professionals who both get paid and can walk away from the problem (or at least pass it on to someone else) to expect families to stay the course. Children however – even those with severe challenging behaviours – are, like everyone else, generally able to respond differently to different situations. We are not the same person at home as we are at work, or out with our friends for a quiet drink. We adopt different roles and are seen differently by other people depending on the situation. There is, of course, always the exception to the rule and those on the autistic spectrum are probably the exception, but then the normal rules do not apply to ASD. For others, as long as there is consistency within the organisation itself (school, home, residential unit, adult day centre, respite centre, etc.) there is a strong chance that positive and lasting change can be effected. It is definitely the case that inconsistency **within** the organisation will strongly mitigate against positive and lasting change.

Consistency is the least that a troubled child can expect from us

Despite all of the children, young people and adults I have known who have displayed a wide variety of challenging behaviours, I have yet to meet one who has wanted to be the way they are, irrespective of their learning difficulty. Challenging behaviours are things they resort to because they haven't found a better way, because we have been unable to teach them a better way. We wouldn't dream of being inconsistent with mealtimes, breaktimes or going home time – why should we be inconsistent with behaviour strategies? We spend vast amounts of time and trouble laying down curriculum documents so that different teachers can offer consistency to our students – why should we tolerate different strategies for behaviour?

Positive

I'm going to grasp the nettle here and get this potentially controversial statement out of the way right at the beginning.

Rewarding good behaviour is a much more effective policy than punishing bad behaviour. Indeed, I would go further in saying that when dealing with challenging behaviour in those who have SLD, PMLD or ASD,[1] we must set our minds against the use of negative responses or punishments, treating them with the greatest possible caution and distrust, and preferably not using them at all.

There are a number of reasons for this.

1   Punishment automatically brings out the negative in us.

2   The use of punishment as an agent of control is open to abuse because it has fear at its centre.

3   Not everybody is able to command the same degree of fear.

4   If we use punishment as a core factor, the behaviour will always surface, because we are waiting for it to happen before we act.

5   Punishing teaches what a person should not do, not what a person should do.

6   Punishment is a short-term solution which may suppress the behaviour but does not resolve it.

7 Punishment is often confused with establishing boundaries, but they are not the same at all.

8 Punishment does not encourage the person to take individual responsibility for their actions.

9 A civilised society is marked by its degree of investment in positive rewards over negative punishments.

CASE STUDY

A number of years ago, when I was just setting out on the road of challenging behaviour discovery (a road I'm still on by the way!) I met Jacky, who came up from our primary site at the age of 11. Jacky was certainly a wild one, quite able – she had a reading age of between 5 and 6 – but very mixed up emotionally and always pushing the boundaries. Teachers struggled to contain her and she inevitably ended up in my office, where I also struggled to contain her. On one particular day after she'd been ejected from the classroom for the fourth time that morning she was sent to my office again but just could not settle. Whatever I threatened her with – withdrawal of all her favourite things and activities – made no difference, in fact it just seemed to hype her up all the more. The final straw came when I withdrew yet another privilege because she wouldn't sit still, upon which she looked me straight in the eye, laughed manically, threw my cup of coffee at the wall (just missing me in the process) and proceeded to trash the room. I totally lost the plot at this point and started shouting back at her with numerous threats including calling her mother *right now*!!

Jacky subsided almost immediately and went into a peculiar state of giggly, twitchy nervousness, half wanting to continue her rampage, half needing to calm herself, all the time pleading with me not to call her Mum, because she would be good, she would be very, very good. Of course I relented (I was always a sucker for a sob story) and of course, Jacky just hyped up again as soon as I backed down. In the end, Jacky's Mum came into school and spoke to us about Jacky, or at least she listened and agreed to talk to Jacky about her behaviour. Jacky was *very* quiet and *very* well behaved throughout the whole interview and it was clear that she was *very* intimidated by her mother.

A number of points come out of this story (apart from the fact that I was asking for trouble by leaving my coffee anywhere near her reach!) and I'll try and relate them to the issues raised above.

Punishment automatically brings out the negative in us

We spend much of our time talking about what pupils, students and adults with SLD, PMLD and ASD cannot do – it's in the titles of difficulties, disabilities and disorders – and although challenging behaviour is couched in terms of what they can do, unfortunately it's that they can be challenging, they can hurt us, they can be troublesome, they can be hard work, they can be problematic! Using punishment as a means of controlling behaviour forces us into that negative spiral; the use of negative language, the raising of voices, the attempts to dominate, the attempts to control, all of which are actually bad for us as educators and carers, because education and care must, by definition, be a positive experience if it is to have any positive effect on the individual. Indeed, merely the emphasis placed on the fact that 'if you **don't** behave/do your work/walk properly you **won't** get your biscuit/go on the computer/turn on the bike' forces both parties into negativity. The mindset is negative because we are looking for the child to be negative. Tim O'Brien notes how the use of negative language can act as a punishment – whether it is deliberately intended to be so or not. For example, he asks:

> *what function does a remark such as 'act your age' perform when directed at a sixteen year old pupil with severe learning difficulties who is presenting with challenging behaviour? What effect will it have on their self-esteem? It does not give any indication of what the pupil should do and due to its personal nature there is a high risk of exacerbating the behaviour. It is also a highly offensive comment to make.*

(O'Brien 1998, p. 77)

Suggesting that using the phrase 'act your age' is a punishment might seem a little extreme, but it is representative of the sort of language that easily creeps in and very easily dominates our thinking. What we need to do is look for the child to be positive, perhaps set up opportunities for him/her to act in positive ways (in this case by acting maturely and responsibly) and then rewarding that positive behaviour.

The use of punishment as an agent of control is open to abuse because it has fear at its centre

I won't go into the numerous details of excesses undertaken in the name of behavioural 'progress' here, but there are many – see for example Murphy and Wilson (1985) and Sturmey *et al.* (1993). And just in case anyone feels that such excesses cannot happen nowadays, Dawn Male (Male 2006) has reported on the findings from a joint investigation into the provision of services for people with learning disabilities in Cornwall, which noted that in 2006, there were:

> *instances of poor and abusive care . . . including staff hitting, pushing, shoving, dragging, kicking, secluding, belittling, mocking, goading . . . withholding food, giving cold showers . . .*

(p. 38)

And this ready escalation has a great deal of logic to it, since to be effective any punishment must be feared by the child. If, however, a particular punishment doesn't work, we will be forced into devising something more fearful that will, and as this battle for control continues, we may end up fearing the child just as much as they fear us. It was certainly the case that we ended up fearing Jacky as much as she feared her mother and perhaps, to a degree, her mother was in this cycle too. That is, we attempt to control the person with learning difficulties; this raises the stakes for the person we're controlling who becomes aggressive; we in turn have to raise the stakes; the person becomes even **more** aggressive; we start to fear the child. We should be liberating children not fearing them.

Not everybody is able to command the same degree of fear

It is evident that what worked for Jacky's mother was never going to work for me, a fact that Jacky established very early on in our relationship. Because Jacky expected punishment to be used to curb her excesses she pushed and pushed until she found the hard place she was used to, one that was way beyond anything I was either willing or able to impose.

If we use punishment as a core factor, the behaviour will always surface, because we are waiting for it to happen before we act

This is a **very** important argument and one that I want to spend a bit of time on. The ultimate aim – the long-term goal – of any behaviour management programme must be to extinguish the undesired behaviour completely, that is, for the person to reject the behaviour as being a fundamental part of their character. But nobody can run before they can walk, perform calculus before they learn how to add 2 and 2, become a valued member of society before they learn how to foster and maintain successful relationships. From small steps, great leaps are made, but we have to teach how to make those small steps first. This means that the pragmatics of any behaviour management programme are about making tiny steps first, and there is bound to be some faltering along the way. This is only to be expected but will not matter greatly if we concentrate on the 'good' behaviour – the behaviour we want the person to adopt – rather than concentrating on the 'bad' behaviour – the behaviour we want the person to lose. If we had rewarded Jacky for her working hard in class for (say) 5 minutes and gradually increased this amount of time as she succeeded we would have been concentrating on the behaviours we wanted Jacky to adopt. Instead we waited for her 'bad' behaviours to occur in order to punish them – we could never, however, punish quite enough.

Punishing teaches what a person should not do, not what a person should do

Learning is hard enough for someone with SLD, PMLD or ASD, without making it harder, especially as there may be **lots** of things that a person (especially one with challenging behaviour) should not do. We therefore end up always punishing and constantly drifting into the negative spiral.

Punishment is a short-term solution which may suppress the behaviour but does not resolve it

Of course the **big** problem with punishment is that it is very likely to work, especially when it is utilised by someone adept at punishing! I'm sure we have all worked (or all continue to work) with someone whose natural inclination is to exercise fear and punishment, for the Wicked Witches of the West exist in all walks of life, not just in Kansas. These are the people who will tell you that you are too soft, that you're pandering to the child, letting him/her get away with murder, letting him/her call all the shots, and that they can control this child without any fancy behaviour management programmes, so just toughen up and get a grip!

Fortunately, punishment cannot be seen as a long-term solution for the very simple reason that it requires the **permanent** presence of a police force. It does not encourage taking individual responsibility. It does not require the individual to want to change, merely to conform when whoever holds the whip is present. When the whip is taken away, or when the person doing the whipping is absent, there is no longer any incentive to maintain a change in behaviour. There can be little doubt that the presence of speed cameras has seriously affected the behaviour of drivers who habitually exceed speed limits – but what happens when you take the cameras away? Are habitual speeders going to continue with their law-abiding behaviour? There was little doubt that Jacky was an angel when her mother was present, but when Jacky came to school without her mother being there, she naturally reverted back to speeding!

Punishment implies that we are waiting for the behaviour to occur. If we wait for the behaviour to occur and then withdraw privileges, the behaviour is exercising all the control.

Punishment is often confused with establishing boundaries, but they are not the same at all

For people with challenging behaviour, boundaries are often incredibly important, especially for those who have an unclear or confused idea of what is expected of them. Boundaries are an opportunity to lay down achievable goals, a chance to apply a limited set of rules that can be gently but consistently applied and often repeated again and again if the person is to have any chance of learning the rules. Jacky was obviously someone who needed boundaries as she was always pushing us to find them, but because we invariably got sucked into concentrating on the negative aspects of her behaviour, Jacky naturally got confused with what we might allow and what her mother might allow. Since there was no way we could keep up with her mother's rigid regime, Jacky was always going to push beyond our boundaries to try and find consistency and we were bound to fail. What we needed to do was establish our own boundaries and reward her for staying within them.

Punishment does not encourage the person to take individual responsibility for their actions

Some may argue that people with SLD or PMLD are not capable of taking that degree of individual responsibility because their learning difficulty precludes it. My experience argues very strongly against this because every single child, young person or adult with challenging behaviours that I have encountered has *wanted* to change, has *wanted* to be loved, has *wanted* to love. Some, a very few, have not been able to, because the effort has been made too late and the behaviour is *so* established it has been impossible to break down within the resources of the school, but this does not alter the basic premise that no child wants to challenge as a natural course of things. They resort to these behaviours as a last resort, because we haven't taught them a better way, because we have failed them.

A civilised society is marked by its degree of investment in positive rewards over negative punishments

I have heard this phrased as 'a civilised society is marked by the degree to which it looks after its most disadvantaged' but essentially, it is the same thing. Certainly one of the things that marks out civilised human societies from animal ones is their willingness to invest time and trouble in persuading individuals to join voluntarily. Animal collectives that require individuals to work together for the benefit of the whole do so either through some form of imprinting – bees, ants, termites, etc. have defined roles that are predetermined, and therefore immutable, before birth – or dominance of one individual in a strict hierarchical order. Meerkats, for example, those lovable creatures that live communally in the African desert, have one dominant female who controls procreation so that only she is allowed to breed – all other females collectively bringing up her young. The control is ruthless, often relying on savage physical punishment that can mean death for any miscreants. Human societies have in the past (and, in some unfortunate cases, the present) also been marked out for their savagery, but hopefully we are moving away from the idea of enforced control. Certainly the UK can count itself one of the most civilised of societies in this respect by the way it 'puts its money where its mouth is' and looks after the most disadvantaged – though of course, there is always more we can do.

Using punishment as a controlling influence is I believe counterproductive, lazy and immoral. Counterproductive because of all the reasons I've outlined above, lazy because it is the easy option that requires no great thought and immoral because it automatically demands that the adult display anger, with the blame laid fairly, squarely and totally on the person with challenging behaviour. But challenging behaviour doesn't happen in isolation, we are part of the challenging behaviour and are responsible because we have failed to teach a better way. Tim O'Brien talks of teaching the child 'spiritual development':

> . . . any progress in a child's learning state is an indication of spiritual progress. Teaching children to develop an incremental awareness of what is within and beyond their own unique experience is a learning process, and must become the responsibility of every teacher.

> (O'Brien 1998, p. 57)

Put another way, the existence of challenging behaviour in a child, young person or adult with learning difficulties is as clear an indication as you would want that (in certain situations at least) they are unable to give or receive love in a way that every human being has a right to. Of course we all lose our temper from time to time, of course we all have little tantrums or occasionally do things we shouldn't do, but generally we should not do these things as a matter of course. Any person who seeks to manipulate or control others in order to get their own way **on an habitual basis** is lacking the ability to express and/or receive love. This is what having a challenging behaviour is about; and punishing a child because they are unable to express and/or receive love is, I would suggest, bizarre, immoral and incredibly uncivilised.

As a conclusion to this section, and without wishing to be too pretentious, this book has largely come about because of my personal deep regret at failing Jacky whilst she was at my school, and there is no doubt that we (or rather I, since I was head of site at the time and therefore solely responsible for instituting behaviour policy and practice) did fail Jacky. I made the decision that because of the extremes of her behaviour, we could not cater for Jacky's needs within the school and put such pressure on the LEA that they were forced to take her off our role and find her a residential placement. They never did find a residential placement; Jacky hardly went to school after she was 14 and she is now in her mid-twenties, a very lost and troubled young lady. I don't know that had I followed the principles that I'm now espousing Jacky would have managed to live to her considerable potential; I don't know, because no-one can know. I do know, however, that I don't want to make those mistakes again.

Reward

It is undoubtedly the case that challenging behaviour can be an extremely powerful tool for the learner. It can often bring instant pay-offs especially in the form of greater attention or immediate withdrawal of problem activities or situations. If punishment has been rejected on both practical and philosophical grounds, the only option is to try and change behaviour using a positive reward system. Although a dictionary definition of 'reward' is:

> *something that is given in return for something done*
>
> (NED 1994),

in behavioural psychology the word 'reward' has a different and very precise meaning. That is, it is:

> *an event which increases the frequency of the behaviour it follows.*
>
> (Ainscow and Tweddle 1988, p. 115)

There are a number of important points which come out of this definition.

1 The term 'reward' is defined in terms of the child's behaviour.

2 It is not a reward if it does not increase the frequency of the desired behaviour.

3 The fact that an adult **believes** something to be rewarding for a person does not mean that it is. I have often heard teachers and TAs talk in terms of rewarding children with catch-all 'rewards' like stars or praise, and whilst these might work for some, they will not work for all. We must, therefore, discover what **motivates** each **individual** person the most and use these as **individual rewards**.

4 Rewards are *not* bribes since a bribe is something offered illegally.

5 Children are not uniform in their need for a reward – it very much depends on their individual circumstances.

6 The need for a reward is no different from the need for help. Some people can learn on their own – some can't.

There are various types of reward; that is primary reward, social reward and activity reward.

Primary reward

Primary here refers to basic need in that these are usually foodstuffs – especially sweets and crisps – and sweet drinks such as Coke. Whilst they can be especially useful in the initial stages of establishing a behaviour and are notably used in the first stages of PECS (Picture Exchange Communication System) (Frost and Bondy 2001), please be *very wary* of using these on two main counts. Firstly, the law of diminishing returns states that the more food rewards you give the less effective they'll be since the person enjoys the tenth sweet, or crisp or sweet drink, much less than the first. Secondly, on pure health grounds, especially diet, as well as the possible adverse effects of sugar and 'E's on behaviour! My general view would therefore be to steer clear of primary rewards in all circumstances.

Social reward

This is essentially praise and attention. How much is down to how well the teacher knows the learner and low-key praise can sometimes be more effective than demonstrative praise – especially if the learner has very poor self-esteem (a distinct possibility with challenging behaviour); but in any event we must be constantly on the look-out for opportunities to praise and give positive attention. Social reward can be given very effectively by others, such as a favourite person or the Headteacher as well as peers, especially if the learner seeks the approval of peers or is feared by them (again, another common consequence of challenging behaviour). Other rewards can supplement social reward but must never replace it, because social rewards have a number of prime advantages in that:

- they tend to be more persistent;
- they can be given immediately and without need for special arrangements;
- they are more easily generalised in learning.

Activity reward

Although these can be 'responsibility rewards' such as taking the register back, ringing the bell for breaktime, etc., they are *much* more effective when they are related to something the learner finds **intensely** motivating. As such, they must be directly related to the individual learner, and as such, you need to know the learner *very* well. For some, especially those with obsessive tendencies and for those on the autistic continuum, such personal rewards can be very powerful and problems often occur in withdrawing the reward when 'time up' is called. (See Chapter 7 'Challenging behaviour and autistic spectrum disorders' for more thoughts on this.) For most, however, the pleasure of the activity reward will be transient and time bound, act as a support to the praise and attention (social reward) naturally given and, if successful, gradually disappear as the new behaviour becomes established. It is important to note that activity rewards should not continue for ever and a day except in the most extreme of cases, but should be gradually faded out over time. We do, after all, want the behaviour to be established as part of the person's new character and not be dependent upon external reinforcers.

In addition to using rewards it is absolutely imperative that we provide constant feedback to the individual, since being told that they are successful is likely to act as an effective additional reward for the learner. To do this we need to ensure that the learner is working at a level that is appropriate to their abilities and needs. In addition, regular feedback also provides the person with an opportunity to (i) learn from mistakes (ii) clarify misconceptions (iii) confirm mastery of certain tasks and (iv) focus on areas that require further attention.

A note of caution on activity rewards

They are, like primary rewards, likely to be subject to the law of diminishing returns, especially if they are being offered once every 20 minutes or so throughout each day. This might not apply to the autistic learner, but could well apply to those with severe learning difficulties. In this case you might have to swap the rewards around on a regular basis, or give open choices (perhaps on a symbols board) so that the learner doesn't get bored and cease to be motivated. It's therefore really important to have an extensive list of strengths and activities that the learner likes (see Chapter 8 'Writing a behaviour management programme').

Common reasons for not offering a reward system

Other kids might get jealous

In an SLD setting at least, it is incredibly unlikely that other pupils will get jealous of one particular pupil receiving a reward for good behaviour when the others are not. At least, I have never personally experienced this phenomenon. The concept of 'fairness' is largely a staff one since SLD pupils seem not to notice, or are more open to the idea of individualised learning than we think. If this does happen, however, you may wish to institute a reward system for all of your pupils – perhaps based on a communal reward at the end of the day (or session) for the whole class behaving appropriately – and, of course, include the pupil who you're rewarding more frequently, thus getting a double opportunity to reinforce the message!

We don't have time to give them a reward

This may often be because rewards often have to be supervised and we're too busy teaching the curriculum. Once again, this comes down to how much you want to change the behaviour. If it's not important enough to warrant the personnel and time input, don't do it. If it is important enough – because the staff and curriculum time are being 'stolen' anyway in containing the behaviour – you have to make the commitment to putting in the resources. Nobody said dealing with severe challenging behaviours was cheap!

It is too disruptive to the rest of the class to give rewards whilst the rest are working

In which case it might be appropriate to leave the room with your charge and find a quiet corner somewhere to give the reward. Even in the most crowded of schools, somewhere can usually be found.

Whilst we will explore the area of what constitutes an effective reward further in Chapter 8 'Writing a behaviour management programme', suffice it to say at this stage that we need to make the new behaviour much more worthwhile to the person with challenging behaviour than the old one by looking for every opportunity to reward good behaviour through the learner's strengths, interests and obsessions.

Control

At the start of this chapter, I talked about **Why?** Let me now refer back to that section to look at the importance of **Control** in the reasons for a person exercising challenging behaviour, especially since many – if not all – challenging behaviours are attempts made by the learner (however crude) to gain some control over their existence.

In the section on **Why?** I made the statement that whatever the actual reasons for the challenging behaviour, for those with SLD at least, all reasons have a tendency to surface as behaviours in one of two broad categories:

1   Task (or situation) avoidance;

2   Attention seeking.

This is largely because these are the two areas where those with severe communication problems and learning difficulties are most likely to be unable to get their personal preferences across. Let us take them separately.

Task avoidance

Task (or situation) avoidance *without* challenging behaviour is largely, if not solely, the prerogative of those who are both able to say 'No' and likely to be listened to when they do so. The bare facts of the matter are that even if those with severe or profound learning difficulties are able to say 'No' they are almost **never** listened to when they do so. As adults living in a relatively free society, we have the right to say 'No' and the reasonable assumption is that our 'No' will be listened to – if not, we have access to rational argument, our freedom to take our physical selves and our labour elsewhere and, if the worst comes to the worst, the law to uphold our claim.

As children living in a relatively free and child friendly society, our children have the right to say 'No' and the reasonable assumption is that even if their wishes are not acted upon, their case will be listened to, heard fairly and honestly by adults who are keen to involve them in a decision-making process and, if the worst comes to the worst, there are at least others in the public purse – social workers, police, child-welfare organisations and, of course, the law – who will listen to their arguments and rationalise any decision.

Do SLD and PMLD adults and children have that same right? Unfortunately '**No!**' Although the theory is that they do have that right, this is not borne out in practice, because as professionals whose job it is to look after the disabled we generally judge that they are not intellectually able to make such decisions. We therefore make those decisions for them, and naturally we judge that it is right that 6-year-old A will get up at 7.00 each morning to get ready for school; 10-year-old B will not punch the nearest person to him whenever he sits in assembly; teenager C will do Drama on a Wednesday morning with the rest of her group; 22-year-old D will have his toenails cut.

And in many ways we are right to make such decisions, because by acceding to their refusals we would be complicit in restricting experiences and learning opportunities. We are after all teachers, parents, carers, etc. and as such it is our duty to broaden experience and teach about social conventions as much as possible. As such there is a natural contradiction between our desire to be understanding and sympathetic to these problems and our need to be practical. Life after all, goes on. It cannot wait for A to wake up naturally – the bus for school will have left for the next pick-up. We all have to do many things we don't want to do – including Drama and assemblies. There are painful consequences of failure to look after our personal care – including in-grown toenails. All of us, both with and without learning difficulties, have to cope with the less pleasant aspects of life and we're not going to help the individual by spoiling them and giving in to tantrums.

We are, however, all individuals. The fact that the majority of us are able to accept the slings and arrows of outrageous fortune does not mean that everybody is able to. For some, the loss of self, the sense of powerlessness, the feeling of being totally out of control is so strong that it takes over and sends them into a panic of violence. It would be like you being asked to eat a bucket of live cockroaches or drink a glass of vomit without the right to say no. What would you do?

CASE STUDY

Rahul is a 14-year-old young man with Angelman Syndrome with considerable communication problems who is operating at around P5. He's a hefty fellow with a considerable clout – and he is beginning to know it. He has a history of occasional violence – usually flapping and slapping – which has always been treated with a sharp telling off and an equally sharp instruction to say 'Sorry' and desist; which was usually enough. As he got older and bigger, however, this tactic met with increasingly less success. Now he will not desist, but continues slapping, sometimes very hard, and is even starting to chase people around the room to get at them. He also harbours grudges and will for weeks, and sometimes months after slap people who have upset him at some time in the past, mostly when they are least expecting it.

Here is a classic case of a young person who is out of control. But I do not mean this in the accepted sense of the phrase. Here is a classic case of a young person **who is out of control because he has no control.** Rahul is being asked (instructed, ordered) to do things he is uncertain of, either because he doesn't understand the instruction, doesn't like the instruction or hasn't had time to process the instruction. He wants to say 'No', but he (physically) can't. He has tried to say 'No' in the past by flapping, but he has been ignored. He has tried to say 'No' in the past by slapping, but this has also been ignored, because he hasn't been able to slap hard enough and has been intimidated by the size and power of adults.

Then gradually, he becomes physically powerful himself and over a period of time recognises his own power. Naturally therefore, he starts to use it.

Now **he** is in a position of power and make no mistake, challenging behaviour is a **very** powerful tool.

Hewett (1998a) has pointed out that challenging behaviour is a term almost exclusively used for those with learning difficulties and if there is one feature which unites all those with severe and profound learning difficulties it is their lack of control over their lives. When considering just the communication problems that those with SLD and PMLD experience every moment of their lives, I am astonished that they don't all have challenging behaviours – a fact that Hewett has also commented on in entitling a chapter 'Challenging behaviour is normal' (Hewett 1998b).

The issue with Rahul was simply resolved, yet it took ages for the school to get there because we were inherently reluctant to give him the control he needed. The objections were very understandable, because giving Rahul that control appeared to contradict a basic 'behaviourist' mantra of rewarding negative behaviour – if you reward negative behaviour, you'll just get more of it. Yet Rahul merely wanted people to listen to him when he said 'No', which is in itself a perfectly reasonable expectation. **It is the behaviour that is unreasonable, not the reason behind the behaviour**. In other words, it is **not** unreasonable that he has the expectation that he will be listened to when he says 'No' but it **is** unreasonable to hit out as a way of saying 'No'. **We have to change his method of saying 'No', not his right to say it or his right to be listened to**.

And this is what we did. We took his flapping as an indication that he wasn't happy, and immediately backed off. He was given choices through a visual timetable, such as doing the activity or doing nothing; working with one particular individual in the class rather than another; waiting for a few minutes before he joined the group (if processing the information was a problem). As a long-term process we experimented with symbol books, especially Clare Latham's recent work in the use of communication books (Latham 2005), all very obvious stuff, but not instituted earlier because the idea of **giving control to children, young people and adults with learning difficulties** – to opt out of lessons, to refuse to do a particular piece of work, to refuse to work with a particular individual, etc. – is so difficult for adults to cope with. And of course, the less control we give, the more likely it is that extremes of behaviour will emerge as being the **only** way that people without a voice will be listened to.

Interestingly, even when the policy had been implemented and had been declared successful, there were still a minority of staff who were targeted by Rahul – despite his severe learning difficulties, he clearly had a good memory for some things. These were always the staff who had had problems in their relationship with him in the past, but they didn't have to do anything specifically wrong – if Rahul was feeling anxious or threatened by something totally unrelated, he would occasionally go out of his way to target them. This created considerable strain in the workplace, because those staff had to make **extra** efforts to be positive towards Rahul – very difficult when he's looking to hit you at every opportunity. Nonetheless, because Rahul was clearly extremely sensitive to what people thought about him, certain staff did have to work extra hard to change their attitudes. Was that an unreasonable demand placed upon them? Perhaps, but we are the teachers, we are the adults, and as such it is our duty to take the mature and grown-up line. If that means working **extra** positively, then maybe that's what we have to do.

Finally under task avoidance, we must be clear that giving an acceptable form of control back to pupils does not, and cannot, mean that the pupil can do anything he/she wants, because we still have a clear responsibility to teach about social norms and conventions; that is, what is socially acceptable. For some children (like Jacky, for example, like Nathan in Chapter 5 'Challenging behaviour and severe learning difficulties', and like several of the children in Chapter 7 'Challenging behaviour and autistic spectrum disorders') who are unable to distinguish between what is socially acceptable and what is socially unacceptable, boundaries have to be established and learning needs to include positive, concrete (rather than abstract) lessons on appropriate and inappropriate behaviours.

Attention seeking

This is also a very common feature of learning difficulties and again, I'm going to make something of a controversial statement when I suggest that **the very best way to resolve attention-seeking behaviour for someone with SLD or PMLD is to give as much attention as the person needs**. On the face of it, this again goes against the received wisdom which tends towards denying attention to 'attention seekers', again on the grounds that you must never reward a negative behaviour. Professional advice on attention seeking within conventionally developing children tends to be confined to very young babies when new parents are red-eyed and sleep deprived by their offspring. Understandably, the sensible thing to do at this stage is to let the baby cry whilst feeds, cuddles, changes, etc. take place at regular and defined intervals so that baby gets used to a regular routine. The advice argues that things are likely to get worse before they get better as baby 'ups the ante' and screams even louder and longer in the expectation that he/she will be picked up and fed, changed, cuddled. Fairly soon, however, baby learns that (i) feeding, changing, cuddling, etc. will occur at regular intervals (ii) they will not take place when the child is screaming or crying and therefore (iii) as there is no additional reward for crying it is not worth the effort. For skilled and practised parents, this strategy is self evident and common sense, and since most workers in SEN will have been parents, it is not surprising that they carry this philosophy through to their dealings with people with SLD and PMLD.

Unfortunately however, people with SLD and PMLD are not conventionally developing children and the lessons learnt by conventionally developing children and their parents cannot always be applied to them! The key point here is that for the vast majority of conventionally developing children, these lessons are learnt early and carry through for the rest of their lives. For a few conventionally developing children these lessons are not learnt (perhaps through poor, over-loving or unstructured parenting) and these will turn into the adults that we all know who are still attention seekers whatever their age – actors, pop stars and drama queens in every walk of life are probably the classic examples. Clearly for people with learning difficulties these are **much** more difficult lessons to learn because all sorts of additional factors come in to play.

1   The learning difficulty itself will mean that lessons fairly easily learnt by conventionally developing children are much harder to learn. It may take considerably greater application and strength from parent(s) who are already suffering from guilt, anxiety and confusion than that demanded in normal circumstances. If that lesson is not learnt early by the child who has learning difficulties it may never be learnt at all.

2   Those of us working with SLD and PMLD know how difficult it can be, even with training and support; how much more difficult is it for parents who don't get that training and support? Being a parent is hard enough, never mind being a parent of a child with severe or profound learning difficulties.

3   The problems of parental bonding with young children with learning difficulties who might not respond in conventional ways are well documented (Nind and Hewett 1994, Ware 2003), suffice it to say that this factor may well cause parents themselves to withdraw affection as a mechanism of self-defence ('If I don't give love I can't be hurt by that love not being returned.') and this in itself might establish unwanted patterns of attention-seeking behaviour.

4   The natural genetic predisposition to learning difficulties – that is that people with learning difficulties are more likely to have children with learning difficulties – is also likely to result in poor parenting skills, in turn resulting in children who are starved of attention and who therefore naturally revert to extreme attention-seeking behaviours.

5   The continual attempts by teachers, support staff, care workers, etc. to apply conventionally developing models to those with learning difficulties (i.e. don't give attention) will only serve to reinforce the starvation of attention. The more you're starved, the more you need and the wilder your actions will be to get what you need.

In these circumstances the only way of successfully combating attention-seeking behaviour is to give the attention demanded. Easy to say – not so easy to deliver, because this carries enormous staffing implications. Essentially, for extreme behaviours at least, we're going to have to provide one-to-one support and how can this be justified? Well, simply by the fact that as with all challenging behaviours, if we don't provide what the person needs – in this case attention – the time will be stolen anyway. Just think of the amount of adult time an attention-seeking person with challenging behaviours takes up – admonishing, telling to be quiet, turning to face the wall, sitting in the naughty chair, expelling from the classroom with a TA to make sure they behave when out of class, making sure they don't wreck their own work or that of others, making sure they don't bully others, etc., etc. These are after all usually the people we **cannot** leave on their own for any length of time because they will **always** resort to behaviours that will gain them attention and the upshot is they often have one-to-one support anyway. More often than not, however, this support is only keeping a lid on the problem, not solving it.

Long-term issues

A further (third) element of **Control** is that it is vitally important that any programme's **long-term** target is for the learner to take control of their own behaviour. This is in many ways like that of an alcoholic or a drug addict – if the person doesn't want to change, they aren't going to change, and we can't force them to change. Many challenging behaviours are, however, an indication of how out of control they are. **We need to look at acceptable ways of giving control to the learner**, so that they are **certain** that by behaving in positive ways they can achieve what the challenging behaviour previously gave them **and** gain our approval into the bargain. That is, that we must convince the person that there is a better way of behaving, better for them and better for us.

Time

Most challenging behaviours can be dealt with relatively simply, quickly and easily by adopting the strategies espoused in this book – but (unfortunately) some may take considerably longer than others!

Challenging behaviour and PMLD

Generally speaking, behaviour management for those who do not have a refined sense of cause and effect – those with profound learning difficulties – is the long haul. Time becomes *the* major feature and it may well take many years to achieve what might be achieved in a matter of months or even weeks with someone higher functioning. This issue is dealt with in considerably more detail in Chapter 6 'Challenging behaviour and profound and multiple learning difficulties'.

There are also additional time factors for those who have a deep-rooted psychosis and psychotic behaviour can occur with those with learning difficulties, though it will probably not be absolutely apparent until late-teens. I don't want to make too much of this, because this is by no means common, though it is likely that every SLD school will have its examples. When an individual's understanding of reality is seriously impaired it is very difficult to apply normal time scales to changing behaviour. When there is the additional factor of learning difficulties thrown in it is virtually impossible. If this is suspected, seek professional help through the local health trust's Clinical Psychology Team. For further reading I would refer you to Emerson (2001) but always remember the following points.

There may be different time scales for success

For those with SLD – irrespective of whether there is an additional ASD diagnosis – **the short-term target should achieve significant success within 4 weeks at the most**. This is not to say that the behaviour will always entirely disappear – behaviours are very powerful agents for many and may serve a number of functions – but even if there are a few lapses, a significant behaviour change should take place. Please remember, however, that **intermittent** failure is part of the learning process and should not be taken as lack of success. Every baby just learning to stand falls over and it is the process of falling over and regaining their balance that leads to the eventual success. If we assumed that the baby had failed every time they fell over, no-one would ever walk, but because we see the regular failures as part of the learning process, we accept each short process of standing up as a mini success. If the initial target does not work, however, don't be afraid to scrap the plan and try a new one. If the worst thing you can do is to give up, the next worst is to hang on to a behaviour management programme that has failed. Go back to the beginning and start again, making sure you have followed the arguments written out in Chapter 8 'Writing a behaviour management programme' since it is very likely that something fairly simple has gone wrong which can be put right reasonably easily.

Make sure that the new behaviour is established before you move on

There is a big difference between initially changing a behaviour and absolutely establishing a new behaviour in its place. The old (challenging) behaviour is likely to have been very important to the individual and it will take time for the new one to become the norm. For those with a severe learning difficulty it might take a considerable time, quite possibly several months, because they have a severe learning difficulty! We need to resist the temptation to push too hard too fast, however tempting it is to do so, whilst continually assessing the situation for the right time to move on to the next short-term target.

Long-term targets

The long-term target is for the learner to take control of their own behaviour and it may take several years of chipping away at the individual behaviours before this can even remotely occur. Do not confuse the short-term and the long-term targets.

Targets will often need to be time bound

This is so that success can be seen to have occurred. The person's learning objective within the behaviour management programme must be within the capability of the learner and often targets are so vague that the learner will **never** achieve them. *To not scream during assemblies* may take a considerable time to achieve, but *to not scream for one minute during assemblies* might be achieved fairly quickly. Going back to babies learning to walk, in challenging behaviour terms, our *first* target for the baby is to stand for 1 second, not to walk unaided. Our second target is for the baby to stand for 2 seconds and so on. In other words we must look for small targets and these should almost always be time bound. If the time is appropriate to the individual we stand a much better chance of being successful.

Time can be the reason Why?

For children, young people and adults who are displaying challenging behaviour in order to gain attention, time is the one thing in demand. That is, the challenging behaviour is displayed in order to gain your time, and the only effective and long-lasting remedy is to give your time. It takes very special people to work with the most severely challenging whilst they're constantly taking chunks out of you – these are the people who **really** deserve to be in the New Year's Honours List. Fortunately for those of us whose responsibility it is to write behaviour management programmes, special schools are full of angels without wings. Managers need to be as brave, recognise their worth, argue the case for one-to-one attention with their LEA and allow the angels to work their magic.

Success

The fact that a programme needs to be successful is so blindingly obvious that it hardly seems to need stating . . . and yet it is quite amazing how often people make behaviour management programmes almost impossible to achieve. Just as success breeds success, so failure breeds failure, despair, resentment, aggression and all of those other negative feelings that we have all faced when dealing with what seems an insurmountable problem. **It is therefore absolutely imperative that attempts to change behaviour are successful**.

In order for this to happen we should **only try to change one behaviour at a time**. Many people who exhibit challenging behaviours have lots of behaviours that they use lots of the time and perhaps for lots of different reasons. It is easy to get overwhelmed with all of these. Don't!! Write down all the behaviours that are problematic and list them in order with the worst being at the top of the list. Think in terms of (i) violence towards you, violence towards other adults, violence towards others with learning difficulties or violence which is self-inflicted – and if there are lots of violent behaviours, which is the worst? Is the punching worse than the pinching or the kicking? Is the hair pulling worse than the spitting? (ii) How frequent is the behaviour? If mild pinching occurs 20 times a day and violent kicking once a term, we will probably be better to concentrate on the less dangerous but more frequent pinching. (iii) Does the behaviour stop the person or other people from learning, from living a safe life, a fulfilling life; does it prevent the person or other people from achieving their full potential?

CASE STUDY

Sean is a 12-year-old boy with Down Syndrome who is operating around P5/6. He has good language skills which he is starting to support with sign, and though he sometimes has difficulty making himself understood (except when he's swearing!) he will generally persevere. He is very fond of those less able than himself, naturally gravitates to those with PMLD and he is especially fond of certain members of staff, particularly Carol, whom he often begs to see 'for a cuddle'.

Sean does, however, get very upset if one of his less able friends is ill, and is especially upset when they have a seizure. He will often imitate their fits, cry, fret, swear very violently and loudly at the injustices of the world, and sometimes hits his head against the wall or floor very hard. He also detests certain lessons and will swear colourfully if forced to do work he objects to, calling whoever is 'making' him do it some very rude and personal names. He will often rip up his own and others' work and tries to run away from the work area and generally disrupt the lesson so that he doesn't have to do what's demanded of him. He likes to flap a tissue or a scarf and will become quite obsessed with this to the exclusion of all else. He gets very upset if this is taken from him. He will sometimes head-bang if he feels people are not listening to him and are forcing him to do the things he doesn't want to do.

When things are going well for Sean he can be a delightful and affectionate boy, but he struggles to adapt to the demands of life generally, and school in particular.

Clearly there are a number of major behaviours here, displayed for a variety of different reasons, and it would be surprising if staff did not feel overwhelmed at times. Just exactly where do you start? In practice, the school decided to write a hierarchy of behaviours thus identifying which one was the worst – in Sean's case, the head-banging, as this was deemed to be the most dangerous. A programme was written to encourage Sean to seek out Carol for a cuddle every time he felt anxious. He would have to ask her permission for a cuddle (which she would never deny) and she initially allowed him to stay with her for about 5 minutes as long as he agreed to go back to his lesson when the time was up. Gradually, this time was reduced, so that after a couple of months, the cuddle was quite brief and the need for it disappeared almost completely.

Once the most severe behaviour was dealt with, the others could be tackled, but staff had to agree to accept all of them without challenge until the worst one could be extinguished. Challenging behaviours often form a very important part of a person's persona – and **we cannot hope to change everything at once**.

We therefore need to accept that we will:

1   Agree on the **worst** behaviour.

2   Concentrate on **one thing at a time.**

3   **Be successful with that one** – only then move on to the next most important.

4   Sometimes that means that academic achievement has to take a back seat.

5   Success can only be achieved if **we** ensure that success is achievable!

Summary

It is vitally important to recognise the contribution of having learning difficulties in the formation of challenging behaviour (Harris *et al.* 1996, O'Brien 1998) since challenging behaviour does not spring up in isolation but is a reaction to circumstances. Having established this, there are seven key areas ('The Magnificent Seven') to concentrate on.

Why?

It may be that we can't find out why – it may be the last straw effect, that the cause is hidden within a cloud of problems or that there are *lots* of problems. For those with SLD or PMLD the behaviour is, however, likely to surface in one of two ways: (i) task avoidance or (ii) attention seeking.

Consistency

A behaviour policy has very little chance of working if everyone is doing their own thing. The best way of achieving consistency is to have collective ownership of any plan. That means that meetings of the *whole group* are **really** important.

Positive

Rewarding good behaviour is a much more effective policy than punishing bad behaviour since it means we have a considerably greater chance of extinguishing the behaviour in the long term. If we wait for the behaviour to occur and then withdraw privileges, **the behaviour is exercising all the control**.

Reward

Challenging behaviour can be an extremely powerful tool for the learner in that it often brings instant pay-offs, especially in gaining greater attention or an immediate withdrawal of problem activities and/or situations. We need to look to reward good behaviour by using the learner's strengths/interests/obsessions, thereby making the new behaviour **much more worthwhile** than the old one.

Control

We need to learn not to be so precious about our own control and trust that children, young people and adults with challenging behaviours can take responsibility. It is vitally important that any programme's **long-term** target is for the learner to take control of their own behaviour. Pupils with SLD and PMLD are likely to spend a very large percentage of their life being controlled by others. It is therefore not much wonder they seek to exercise control in the only way they can. **Everyone** has the right to say 'No'. **Everyone** has the right to be listened to when they say 'No'. Taking away that right is not the answer. Teaching a better way is. A way that is both positive and rewarding for the learner is far more likely to have both short-term and long-term benefits for everyone.

Time

Don't expect a short-term solution with those who have PMLD and challenging behaviour. Patience, care, love and time are probably going to be the only answers. For those whose challenging behaviours are related to needing attention, your time and love are the most important gifts you can bring to them.

Success

Start with small steps – don't be too ambitious. Concentrate on **one thing at a time** by agreeing on the **worst** behaviour. Be successful with that one – only then move on to the next most important. Success can only be achieved if we ensure that success is achievable! If the learner has SLD, the behaviour should start to change within 4 weeks **at the most**; if it hasn't – rip up the programme and try another tack.

Please remember

For the vast majority of children, young people and adults with SLD or PMLD, behaviours which challenge adults are not premeditated or intended to have any particular outcome other than, in the broadest sense, 'give me attention' or 'take me away from this'. They are, rather, reflections of the person's difficulties in understanding how they can fit in with the many complex routines that make up ordinary life (Harris 1995).

Notes

1   There may be room for punishment within higher functioning ESBD and mainstream learners – though not according to Tim O'Brien! (O'Brien 1998) – but as this is not a book about ESBD or mainstream learners and as I profess no skill in either area, I am not in a position to say.

CHAPTER 5

Challenging behaviour and severe learning difficulties

SLD teaching and mainstream teaching are different

In Chapter 2 'What are SLD and PMLD?', we talked about a working definition of 'severe learning difficulties' and stated that most learners with SLD (certainly those in SLD schools) will be functioning at an intellectual level equivalent to conventionally developing 2 to 5-year-olds (around P4 to Level 1 of the National Curriculum). All of those defined as having SLD will have (often very severe) communication difficulties, and all will have problems with learning – especially in retaining information, maintaining concentration and understanding abstract concepts.

Clearly these problems are significant and it is perplexing, to say the least, that successive governments have refused to reinstate the option of specific special needs training at student teacher level, preferring instead to hide behind the frankly preposterous fallacy that the National Curriculum fits all. It is not possible to simply 'dumb down' from mainstream and expect teaching to be effective because those with SLD learn in a totally different way from their mainstream counterparts. The refusal to take this point seriously has inevitably led directly to a running down and closure of SEN departments at universities and a consequent diminution in specific research on how people with SLD learn.

The wholesale shipping in of mainstream teaching initiatives (such as the National Numeracy and Literacy Strategies) has often been echoed in the general attitude towards problem behaviours in SLD, especially in the philosophy that the behaviour is somehow independent of the learning difficulty and needs to be addressed as a separate issue. The facts do, however, lead us to the inevitable conclusion that it is quite the opposite. It is indeed vitally important to remember that people with severe learning difficulties who have challenging behaviours, display those challenging behaviours **because** they have severe learning difficulties! If this seems an obvious statement to you, then good, because that's one less reader I have to convince of the fundamental correlation between the learning difficulty and the behaviour.

Several points emerge from this.

We cannot automatically transfer mainstream behavioural strategies

Children, young people and adults with SLD need to be taught how to behave appropriately just as they need to be taught how to cross a minor road, know that

£1 buys more than 50 pence, switch on a kettle safely, ask appropriately for more of a favoured object, use the toilet independently; and they need to be taught in ways that are sympathetic to their individual learning styles. It is not possible merely to transfer strategies that are effective with a conventionally developing 1-year-old, 3-year-old, 5-year-old, etc. and expect them to be effective, any more than it is possible to teach Maths to children with SLD using the National Curriculum and the National Numeracy Strategy (Cutler 2000, Robbins 2000, Staves 2001) or to teach SLD children to read using phonics (Gibson 1989, Lorenz 1998, Lacey 2006).

Total behavioural independence may not be possible

Clearly for children, young people and adults with SLD who consistently display challenging behaviours, whatever teaching methods we have been using have not worked, otherwise lessons would have been learnt. It may be that it is outside of their abilities to learn the lessons completely, just as it might be outside of their abilities to cross a minor road independently, but we are still obliged to teach to the maximum of their abilities whatever they may be. Whilst this may mean that we will **always** have to give some support to some learners in their behavioural learning – in exactly the same way that we might always have to give some support to some learners in their road crossing lessons – it does not mean that we can stop trying to teach the appropriate way to behave. We may come to the decision that it is not in the learner's best interests to waste time on trying to teach him/her how to cross a road independently if he/she doesn't have the intellectual ability to recognise that a car may hurt him/her, but it does not mean that we should stop trying to teach road skills, merely that the target needs revising, to say, learning to stop at a kerb without a prompt. In the same way, we cannot abandon behavioural learning because the learner is unable (for whatever reason) to behave appropriately totally independently.

Behavioural success is about much more than mere containment

For some children, young people and adults with SLD, teaching how to behave appropriately may be of primary importance and these lessons may take over a large part of the normal weekly timetable. For a few, teaching how to behave appropriately may take over the **entire** weekly timetable. Those who display challenging behaviours to such a degree that they require constant one-to-one (or even two-to-one) attention are not uncommon in SLD schools. Yet equally commonly, these children are 'contained' in the sense that the expectations are that the one-to-one (or two-to-one) support prevents damage to other children, adults and property. Success is measured in the number of times that the behaviours do not hurt anyone or anything (except possibly the one-to-one!), rather than the idea of the challenging behaviours being replaced by other behaviours which serve the same purpose but are not aggressive or anti-social. This is not usually because nothing has been tried, but paradoxically because too much has been tried. In many cases we have tried to teach children, young people and adults with SLD about appropriate behaviour as though they didn't have a learning difficulty!

Teaching behaviour may become (in the short term at least) *the* curriculum

If we recognise that the teaching of some children, young people and adults with SLD who consistently display challenging behaviours may take up a major part, or even all, of the weekly timetable, it naturally implies that **all other learning is of secondary importance**. If other learning takes place, all well and good, but this cannot and must not be of prime importance until the behavioural issues have been satisfactorily dealt with. For schools and other inspected institutions, this means that managers and teachers must be brave enough to suspend expectations of other 'normal' learning taking place until the challenging behaviours are sufficiently resolved to enable the individual to 'step back' into society. There is no reason to believe that Ofsted would not support such a practice **where the challenging behaviour is sufficiently severe and where strong behavioural policies and practices are in place**. There is, in fact, an incredibly strong argument for maintaining that the *Every Child Matters* document (HMSO 2003) states that we should do just that.

We have to establish effective ways to teach behaviour

Although it is imperative that we teach appropriate behaviour in the same way as we teach every other area of the curriculum (that is, in a way that is commensurate with the learning style of the individual) we cannot teach it as a discrete subject as we would teach Maths, English, Science, etc. With this in mind, I have turned to work previously carried out by John Harris, in order to provide an entirely appropriate vehicle for delivering an SLD National (Behavioural) Curriculum!

As a final addendum to this chapter's introduction, please note that the correlation between the learning difficulty and the behaviour does not rule out the need to stay closely within the confines of 'The Magnificent Seven' and I will make constant reference back to these over the next few pages.

Focus on practice

In the mid-nineties John Harris embarked on a research project in the West Midlands which involved a number of SLD schools (Harris 1995, Harris *et al.* 1996). This involved a clear focus on the existing and established practice which the schools then pooled to come up with a 'top ten'. All of these strategies were both effective and popular with staff and are as relevant today as they were then. The top ten are:

1 Help the learner to establish positive relationships with one adult.

2 Formalise judgements about appropriate and inappropriate behaviour using a system of rewards.

3 Introduce planned activities matched to the learner's strengths and weaknesses.

4 Focus on teaching language and communication.

5 Encourage language and communication for meeting individual needs in everyday settings.

6 Help the learner to anticipate the sequence of daily events and activities.

7 Provide opportunities for the pupil to opt out of activities.

8 Convey staff expectations clearly and provide consistent feedback.

9 Ensure that all staff are aware of the agreed methods of working.

10 Provide a written protocol which describes how to respond to each challenging behaviour.

We shall now focus on each one of these areas individually.

1 Help the learner to establish positive relationships with one adult

CASE STUDY

When Tina first went to her secondary SLD school aged ten she was already around 5'8'' and built like a Russian shot putter from the 1960s, big, strong and very muscular. She had been transferred early from the primary school in the same LEA because she had become an extreme danger to the smaller and more vulnerable children around her. Tina had severe learning difficulties, severe communication problems, very limited powers of concentration and was operating intellectually at around 2 years old (P5). She was also, however, bubbly, full of life and often very loving.

Tina's standard behaviours were to slap, punch, kick, bite, and/or spit at, and/or pull the hair of, and/or throw the nearest object to hand at anybody who happened to be within reach or within spitting/throwing distance. Such actions were usually accompanied by manic laughter and hyperactivity. Naturally the school tried to find out why, but there did not seem to be any particular triggers, or at least, we were unable to find the triggers. There were no particular times of the day or particular lessons where she did this more. Her actions did not seem to relate to how she had been at home or any monthly cycles, since even though she was only ten her physical development indicated that she may well reach puberty early. Interestingly, her mother had died when she was quite young; her father had married again but it was known that there were difficulties in Tina's relationship with her stepmother (not surprisingly given Tina's behaviours); and Tina would often burst into tears and cry inconsolably, especially after she had 'lost it' for no apparent reason at all. If there was a consistency in her anti-social behaviours it was that she nearly always targeted her favourite adults and hurt them the most. It would only take her a couple of seconds to turn a friendly cuddle into a full-blown attack.

Tina's physical strength was considerable, even at ten, and she often hurt staff to such a degree that the frequent bruises, weals and scars that appeared indicated that somebody else had been 'Tina'd'. Although staff had been trained in restraint techniques, the suddenness and violence of the attacks meant that they were understandably very wary of her and, as a result, staff had to spend more time working out if she was going to blow than actually getting to know her.

Step forward Brenda, who, supported by other members of staff, volunteered to be Tina's permanent one-to-one and was with Tina all day, every day for a year or more. During that time Brenda took everything that Tina could throw at her and gave Tina back certainty, security, affection, warmth and, most of all, love. During that time, Tina learnt that Brenda would always be there for her no matter what she did and Brenda learnt about Tina as no other member of staff was able to. I'm sure there were a number of times when Brenda silently (and sometimes not so silently!) cursed Tina and the world in general, but over time, she became **the** expert on Tina, so that we all got to know her so much better. Progress was not smooth by any means and there were often doubts as to whether the school was the appropriate place for Tina (rather than a residential setting) but because Brenda stuck in there, small successes definitely took place. The frequency and ferocity of the attacks slowly diminished; Brenda was able to step away and let other staff in to take over the main one-to-one support; and gradually even the need for one-to-one support receded.

It is now (at the time of writing) six years after Tina initially came to school, and she is (almost!) a model pupil. She no longer has anyone allocated to her for behavioural support and although she still does sometimes blow, it is a rare occurrence (certainly less than once a term) and usually towards the end of the term when we are all knackered anyway. Tina is undoubtedly the success story of the school, but this relationship between success and establishing a positive relationship with a single member of staff (who will virtually always be a TA) is by no means unique.

How did establishing positive relationships with Tina and (at least) one staff member fit in with Why?, Consistency, Positive, Reward, Control, Time and Success?

Why?

Working that intensively with any learner allowed Brenda to know Tina as well as anyone could. Whilst we still may not have been able to say with absolute certainty why Tina behaved in the way that she did at the times that she did (though in hindsight, an educated guess would be related to needing attention) Brenda's deep knowledge and understanding was undoubtedly central to Tina's success.

Consistency

Brenda was able to set the tone for others' work with Tina. She was respected by the other staff for putting her neck on the line and was able to show that a firm but gentle approach actually worked.

Positive

Establishing that initial positive relationship gave all other members of staff the confidence and certainty to pursue a similarly positive line, rather than being fearful of the behaviour and reacting negatively to it.

Reward

Having had so many 'failures' in her short life, Brenda's unconditional love clearly struck a very strong chord with Tina, even though there were almost as many steps back as forward in the short term.

Control, Time and Success

Focusing on developing one, strong, positive relationship moved the school's focus away from short-term crisis management. There is no doubt that it did take time (6 years is a long time to teach just one part of the curriculum) but without the self-control that Tina now undoubtedly has, her life – especially when she leaves school in 3 years' time – would be very different.

What can we learn from helping Tina to establish positive relationships with one adult?

Oddly, given that I'm lauding Brenda as being someone exceptional (which she is!), it is very important not to feel inadequate, lacking or unprofessional, if you can't get on with a particular learner. It happens to us all – even to Brenda. This is especially true of behaviours where personal confrontation occurs, or where extreme behaviours are apparent, such as spitting, hair pulling, biting, punching, pinching, etc., but it could equally just be that you don't particularly like someone, or are lacking in empathy for that particular person. Don't beat yourself up over it, as long as you're not lacking in empathy for all of your pupils and as long as you keep **trying** to turn any negatives into positives. The aim should be for one volunteer who can pass on his/her success to others, and for the rest of us to support him/her as much as we possibly can. Working with SLD is very much about working as part of a team and it is incredibly important that this team ethos is maintained.

2 Formalise judgements about appropriate and inappropriate behaviour using a system of rewards

> ### CASE STUDY
>
> Nathan is 10 years old, has SLD and Down Syndrome, is operating developmentally around P6 (2–3 years old in conventional terms) and is probably the naughtiest boy in the world. It's not that he does anything majorly bad, though he does have a tendency to bully other, less forthright, children, it's more that he has hundreds of low-level 'irritations' and is always doing things he's not supposed to do. He's quite a bright boy, and has the potential to achieve quite a high level of independence, but (as one staff member noted) he has 'the concentration levels of a distracted goldfish'!
>
> As Nathan comes into school in the morning, all beaming smiles and angelic charm, saying 'Good morning' to everyone he passes, he will have committed several naughty acts in the 20 seconds it has taken to go from the bus to the class, even though a member of staff is holding his hand all the time. A typical such walk will have seen him goose the bus escort as she bends over to unstrap another child; poke his tongue out at another boy he often bullies; pull a picture off a corridor wall display; try to dash into a classroom that's not his; pinch an apple from the breaktime fruit bowl; insist upon getting a cuddle from one of his favourite TAs and then turn that cuddle into something that's far too sexual for a 10-year-old – and this is all before he's even set foot in the classroom!

One of the side effects of this type of behaviour – again so typical within SLD schools – is that there is a very strong natural tendency to be negative with everything Nathan does. That is, because he's **always** being naughty, we're **always** telling him off. Nathan says 'Sorry' 352 times in the average day with an appropriate and totally sincere **look** of contrition, which you **know** he doesn't mean. Worse, there is also a tendency to be overly repressive and use **lots** of incredibly negative language with the facial expressions to go with them. How many times does Nathan hear: 'Don't'; 'Stop'; 'Bad'; 'How dare you do that?'; 'What do you think you're doing?'; 'Turn and face the wall'; 'Say you're sorry'; 'I'm not going to be your friend if you're going to do *that*', etc. etc.? And because Nathan hears them so many times from so many people, they become meaningless and only serve to lock **us** into a negative spiral.

If we're going to formalise judgements about appropriate and inappropriate behaviour using a system of rewards, we have to decide what is appropriate. Nathan knows a lot about the inappropriate, because he's always being told about that, but how can we reward appropriate behaviour when this might only last for a few seconds at a time, and is probably accidental anyway because Nathan hasn't spotted anything naughty to do . . . yet!

Clearly Nathan's level of learning difficulty is the key, and equally clearly the policy that's been used with Nathan (of using negative language, particular tones of voice, disapproving facial expressions and body language) has not worked because to a large degree these are abstract concepts. To a large degree language itself is an abstract concept and we have already established that people with SLD find it very difficult to learn from abstract concepts. We wouldn't dream of teaching Nathan about the ancient Egyptians by simply reading to him from a book. We would have to dress him up as an Egyptian, eat real Egyptian food, build a model pyramid, bandage him from head to foot like a mummy, support him in making a model of the Nile delta, etc. And we wouldn't just do these things once, but several times, so that he can learn by repetition. In other words we will teach Nathan using concrete real objects so that he can have first-hand experience of what it is we want him to learn, and then we'll teach these lessons again. In other words, we will adapt our teaching to fit in with his severe learning needs. But why don't we do the same with behaviour? Well perhaps the problem is in the number and variety of behaviours which Nathan exhibits. Where do we start?

How about at the beginning – with **Why?**

Why?, Consistency, Positive, Reward, Control, Time, Success

With Nathan, the behaviours were so frequent that it was a bit pointless doing any observations – you couldn't write quickly enough! – but a home visit indicated that there were a number of problems relating to forming primary bonds. Nathan had a room of his own, but there was nothing in it – no toys, no games, no books. His mother, a refugee and on her own, found Nathan as difficult as we did and overcame the problem by ignoring him, or putting on one of Nathan's favourite videos and expecting him to watch that whilst she cooked, cleaned or did some other domestic chore. She couldn't take him out because she couldn't control him and so most of their time together was spent in a pretty bare flat getting bored. She wanted to love Nathan, but didn't know how, because his learning difficulties and challenging behaviour perplexed her so much.

This seemed to indicate that Nathan's troubles were largely about attention seeking, though there were undoubtedly some task avoidance issues as well, because Nathan had no discipline or structure and had not learnt to concentrate on new tasks. We therefore had to supply **consistent** and **positive** concrete learning opportunities. This we did by explaining the task – in the first instance, to walk from the bus to the class without interfering with anyone or anything (with one-to-one support) – and then actually doing it . . . again and again and again and again until he got it right; and since it took six goes to even get off the bus the first time, and then we had to continually go back to the start every time he interfered with someone or something along the way, you can imagine that this took some time. There was, however, no need for telling off at any time, or any other negative verbal or body language, because as soon as he did something inappropriate he was merely walked back to the start. The learning was all in the actual event. Nathan's **reward** was in finally reaching his classroom, and receiving *lots* of fulsome praise for his achievement, since he was (and still is) an incredibly social boy who really loves school and the people in it.

For Nathan the issue of **control** was more about an extreme confusion about expectations – what was expected of him and what he had to do to gain affection – rather than his anxiety about not being in control. Nathan's (and our) problems stemmed from Nathan having never learnt self-control, and our task was to teach him without resorting to negative tactics.

With the initial success came a gradual moving away from the need to behave perfectly for a **short time** (say 30 seconds) and moving on to the expectation that he would behave *reasonably* well over a **longer time** (say 30 minutes) which then attracted a separate **reward** of a 10-minute computer game. Occasional misbehaving can be tolerated much more easily simply because it is occasional and although there are still times when we need to tighten up again, these instances are fewer as Nathan gradually acquires greater self-control. **Success** is, of course, relative (to where Nathan started from) and complete success, where Nathan needs no behavioural support in or out of the classroom, is still a long way off, but we can say the same about his road-crossing, shopping or language skills. Taking complete self-control of his own behaviour is a long-term target, but that mustn't distract us from the immediately achievable shorter-term goals.

What can we learn from formalising judgements about Nathan's appropriate and inappropriate behaviour using a system of rewards?

1 We needed to establish a hierarchy of behaviours so that the most severe were dealt with first. In Nathan's case, this was judged on the frequency of the low-level behaviours which stopped him from accessing any other learning, rather than the more aggressive, but much less frequent, bullying.

2 Nathan needed to understand what was expected of him and recognising that he has severe learning difficulties, the instructions had to be kept both simple and achievable – as in 'Walk to the classroom'.

3   We had to establish clear and understandable boundaries about what is acceptable and what is unacceptable – as in 'Don't touch anyone or anything'.

4   Having kept instructions simple we had to establish with Nathan that actions have consequences – as in 'We will *always* go back to the start if you don't follow the instructions'.

5   Praise is always the best reward but can be supported by material (activity) rewards – in Nathan's case being part of the classroom group and having 10 minutes on the computer.

6   Whilst we needed to remember that the long-term aim must be for self-controlled behaviour, in Nathan's case we had to teach him how to control himself for very short periods (initially for 30 seconds, then for a minute, then for 5 minutes and so on) before we could have any expectation that he might achieve some degree of behavioural independence.

3 Introduce planned activities matched to the learner's strengths and weaknesses

> **CASE STUDY**
>
> Mohammed and his family arrived in the UK from a North African country ravaged by successive civil wars when Mohammed was four. Initially he went to a mainstream nursery for assessment, but it was very quickly apparent that he was not going to cope, and he was transferred to an SLD school by the age of five. Preliminary observations revealed a very disturbed child who was unable to settle into a classroom setting and who was proving to be very challenging. It was quite difficult to work out his academic abilities since they were hidden within the welter of behaviours, but independent educational psychological reports assessed his receptive language as quite good, though his expressive language was very delayed even in his first language. There had been suggestions that he was on the autistic continuum, since he displayed a number of 'autistic-like' behaviours – particularly repetitive and obsessional behaviours – though he has not, to date, been diagnosed and there are no suggestions that he will be. In any event, Mohammed appears to have major problems with (i) sensory integration[1] in that he seems to be very easily over-stimulated and (ii) communicating his basic needs. These factors (and perhaps other unknown issues) appear to cause him **considerable** anxiety. That anxiety can very quickly spiral out of control when he may slap his face, head-bang against walls, run wildly about the room, scream very loudly, vomit constantly, strip off his clothes and occasionally be violent towards others.

It became apparent fairly soon that Mohammed needed a calm, ordered, secure structure where there was a minimum amount of stimulation and where he was absolutely confident that his basic needs would be met. This was made even more apparent when his class went on a school trip for a week in his first summer term without taking Mohammed, since his behaviours would have been impossible to manage outside of school – and Mohammed had a wonderful time! By the Tuesday with the whole class to himself, his anxiety levels had dropped right down – indicated by his calmness and lack of stress-related behaviours. Various staff were able to work much more productively with him than previously, concentrating on sensory integration, Cooking and Swimming – the latter two subjects being particular favourites of his.

Why?, Consistency, Positive, Reward, Control, Time, Success

Although the specific reasons for Mohammed's myriad and sometimes quite bizarre behaviours will probably never be known, within the school context the **Why?** seemed to relate very strongly to task avoidance. Or rather, Mohammed was reacting adversely to doing a task which involved so many other children, with so many other adults, with so much noise and (to him at least) extremes of sensory confusion. In other words, Mohammed was reacting negatively to a fairly typical SLD classroom. He desperately needed a quieter, calmer environment where staff could be both **consistent** and **positive** in their approach with him rather than fighting with him all the time. Here, the **reward** for Mohammed is in the actual process of taking him out of the classroom where sensory overload is much more easily controllable. Mohammed is therefore in much more control over the things that really cause him stress – largely, other people. Once the short-term target – to significantly reduce his anxieties – has been achieved, small amounts of **time** can be devoted to the longer-term target of gradually reintroducing him into the classroom, especially for activities that he really enjoys, like Cooking and Swimming. **Success** for Mohammed can probably only be achieved by recognising his learning needs and acting accordingly.

What can we learn from introducing planned activities matched to Mohammed's strengths and weaknesses?

Working to Mohammed's strengths, particularly his ability to work productively in a quiet and calm environment, gave us a much more positive view of Mohammed. Establishing exactly what a particular person's strengths are may also give good pointers for rewards, distractions and activities to be used for establishing appropriate behaviours, especially when so much of the time with people with challenging behaviours can be spent on the negative. It's so much better working with what people can do, rather than battling to get them to do what they can't do. By all means move on – but do it very slowly; don't make it difficult to succeed (in fact make it as easy as you possibly can) and build slowly on the success you have achieved.

4 Focus on teaching language and communication

Without exception, every single example and case study quoted in this book has been about communication, or at least, the inability to communicate about needs and wants successfully. The communication difficulties experienced by people with SLD is a theme which permeates the whole nature of challenging behaviour and given the level of frustration derived from an inability to make needs or wants understood, it's surprising there's not more of it.

Generally speaking, focusing on teaching language and communication is what SLD schools do very well. There is, of course, never enough Speech and

Language Therapy and it has always struck me as ludicrous that schools have no control over the level of therapeutic input (including physio and occupational therapy), especially when such therapy can be an essential part of the Statement of Special Educational Need. I can't help coming to the conclusion that when the provision of the essential therapies works in schools, it does so despite the system rather than because of it.

Having said that, however, the majority of SLD schools that I know of tend to operate a 'total communication system', do not rely exclusively on either written or spoken language and support these well with sign, gesture, symbol (including such systems as PECS), ICT systems, medium-tech communication aids such as the 'Step-by-Step' and 'BigMac' switches, photographs, objects of reference and occasionally touch cues.

In challenging behaviour terms there are, however, two major issues that arise out of teaching communication: firstly, there is little point in concentrating heavily on communication, if we refuse to listen or allow that person to say 'No' or 'I don't like that' and secondly, like the teaching of Maths, the communication skills imparted must be of practical use to the individual in giving them control over their environment and their relationships with others. This leads us on to the next of John Harris's top ten.

5 Encourage language and communication for meeting individual needs in everyday settings

An area of challenging behaviour which I haven't mentioned until now, but which is undoubtedly common within all SLD settings, is extreme passivity. Whilst one end of the spectrum of passive challenging behaviour is I suppose the elective mute – which is interestingly attributed to 'emotional disturbances' by Kiernan *et al.* (1987) – selected silences, withdrawals, extreme avoidance techniques, etc. would appear to stem from a combination of lack of confidence that the right answer can be given, a physical inability to communicate, an intellectual inability to communicate and, quite possibly, a lack of something to communicate about.

In these circumstances the need to encourage practical language and communication skills for meeting individual needs in everyday settings becomes paramount and some exciting work is currently being done by Nicola Grove and Keith Park both individually (Grove 2005, Park 2004) and together through their 'Storytracks' initiative www.storytracks.com. Their theory is that whilst children with SLD and PMLD do **listen** to stories almost as much as non-learning-difficulties children, the severe communication problems experienced by these children preclude the art of **telling** stories. Stories are essential to the communicative development of the child because they teach us to listen carefully; they teach us about structure, and about the natural rhythms and flow of language; they teach us about emotions – fear, excitement, anxiety, heartbreak, happiness, love – in a safe and secure setting, not only other people's (the characters' in the story line), but most importantly, our own. 'Storytracks' is an attempt to develop story-telling skills in children, young people and adults with SLD and PMLD through telling very simple, but dramatic stories, initially by the adult (or leader of the group if working with adults with learning difficulties). Over time, learners are encouraged to take in not only the structure and essential elements of that particular story, but also the structure and essential elements of story-telling itself. They can then move on to the most important part – telling their own stories, telling their own lives.

If I've had a particularly bad weekend and I come into work on Monday even more grumpy than I normally am, it helps considerably if I can unburden my angst to a friend who I know will be sympathetic – a trouble shared is a trouble halved. But in order to be able to do that I have to know how to tell a story – I have to be able to communicate the essential elements in a relatively short space of time, keeping it interesting and holding the attention of my listener. But this involves quite complex story-telling skills learnt as a child by constant repetition of such stories as 'Little Red Riding Hood' or the 'Three Little Pigs'. You have to be able to tell these stories (again and again and again) before you can hope to even vaguely master the art of describing what happened to your weekend. Those with SLD **listen** to these stories, but they don't **tell** them, because the art of telling a story has never been taught, because the communication difficulties are too great. No they're not – look up 'Storytracks'!

Why? Consistency, Positive, Reward, Control, Time, Success

The severe communication difficulties which those with SLD face on a daily basis are almost the answer to **Why?** on their own – but they are even more immediately apparent when translated into attention seeking – the need to form safe, secure and lasting relationships – and task avoidance – the need and right to say 'No'. The **consistency** relates to our abilities to teach functional communication skills which step beyond the mere acquisition of language and the joy of being able to communicate effectively is a **reward** in itself. Whilst effective communication skills may not automatically transfer control to the communicator it is undoubtedly true that the lack of communication skills goes a long way to ensuring a lack of **control,** and any **time** invested in improving communication skills is almost bound, by definition, to breed **success** in reducing the incidence of challenging behaviour.

6 Help the learner to anticipate the sequence of daily events and activities

One of the very positive aspects of the increase in autism awareness is the increased use of visual timetables and the general recognition that people with SLD also often have considerable problems in flexibility of thought and coping with change. This issue is dealt with in detail in Chapter 7 'Challenging behaviour and autistic spectrum disorders' but in short I would strongly advocate this strategy on the grounds that it (i) takes away confusion by giving order, certainty and structure to the day, especially through regular joint reference to the timetable should that be needed and (ii) reduces anxiety, and therefore stress, and therefore expressions of challenging behaviour.

7 Provide opportunities for students to opt out of activities

This case raised two interesting points. Firstly, there is no doubt that Christine's behaviour was very manipulative but why bother to adopt a strategy of providing opportunities for her to opt out of activities when she was already doing it herself very successfully. Secondly, the natural instinct was to resist her attempts to manipulate; to suggest that everyone has to stay in class so why shouldn't she; to object to her sitting in the Head's room colouring; to object to her being picky about when (and indeed if) she was going back to class.

Why? Consistency, Positive, Reward, Control, Time, Success

Clearly Christine had a problem with staying in class, and equally clearly the **Why?** related, at least on her bad days, to task avoidance. On these bad days, it didn't seem to matter what the task was – she was going to avoid it. Further, it didn't seem to matter how **consistent** we as staff were, because it very much depended on her own state of mind – what had happened yesterday; what had happened the night before; what had happened that morning; what had happened on the bus; how she was feeling physically. We could continue to be **positive**, but Christine would engineer a confrontation – she was very adept at that – and once the argument had started, it didn't matter what **reward** we would offer, it was never going to be enough. The key factor was therefore **control** and because Christine felt overwhelmed by being out of control (that is, not in control) she exercised control in the only way she knew how – through behaviour which challenged. And, of course, it worked, because she knew that we couldn't make her physically stay in the class, we couldn't physically make her do the work; we couldn't physically make her do anything she didn't want to do.

What Christine was saying was:

That's it. You're all a bunch of *** and I don't give a *** what you want you *** lousy ***. I don't care, I don't care, you can all *** yourselves.

What Christine was communicating was:

This is too difficult for me and I'm very frightened that I'm going to fail (again!). I've spent my whole life failing and I don't want to do it any more. I'm going to leave the classroom now and go to somewhere I feel safer.

And if it was put this way, would we not all feel tremendous sympathy for Christine and bend over backwards to allow her to leave the place of fear and go to her safe place? But Christine has severe learning difficulties, and **cannot** express herself in this way, she can only f and blind and hit out and rant and rail against the world. She desperately needs some control over what is happening to her, but knows of no other way to get it. We cannot (we must not) deny her the control, but we cannot (and must not) let her continue with her anti-social, manipulative, dangerous and challenging behaviour. We therefore have to teach her a better way of exercising that much needed control. Once Christine has learnt that she can leave the classroom whenever she wants to, whenever she feels too stressed or anxious or fearful, she can over **time**, be rewarded for staying in the class for initially (say) 10 minutes. She is much more likely to survive for the 10 minutes, even on a bad day, because she is certain that she can leave simply by asking (or pressing a BigMac which says 'Get me out of here', or holding up a red card, or flap like Rahul in Chapter 4 in the section on 'Control'). The objection often voiced to this strategy is that the likes of Christine are being rewarded for negative behaviours (i.e. not staying in the lesson), but we are, of course, rewarding Christine for not exhibiting challenging behaviours in order to exercise control – an entirely different proposition. In other words we are not objecting to the exercise of the control, merely the (anti-social) means Christine employs. The **success** is, therefore, in teaching Christine a better way of exercising control, and once that is established we can work on getting her to stay in class for longer by using the normal system of rewards.

What can we learn from providing opportunities for Christine to opt out of activities?

It teaches an alternative to opting out by using inappropriate behaviours. Despite the oft-voiced belief that this is open to abuse, it is my experience that it is seldom if ever taken advantage of because SLD children, young people and adults intrinsically enjoy and want to be part of a group. They all want to succeed, and they all want recognition of that success. Even those with ASD who have no interest in social approbation will not take advantage, if it is explained that these are the rules and everyone has to abide by the rules. Only when we have tackled the problem of opting out acceptably, can we begin to tackle other issues, such as (in Christine's case) how long she can be expected to stay in class before being rewarded, and as a general rule we must always begin short and progress long. In other words, it makes sense to initially expect seconds rather than minutes so that success is made easy not hard.

8 Convey staff expectations clearly and provide consistent feedback

This is again an issue of communication, but more about our communication skills than the learner's. It is especially related to how we structure and order any behaviour management programme and how we relate that programmeback to the learner. Challenging behaviour can often occur – and programmes can often break down – because we fail to be clear and specific with learners about what is expected of them. This issue is dealt with much more comprehensively in Chapter 8 'Writing a behaviour management programme', but some points are worth mentioning now.

1   The learner must understand what is expected of him/her, so use any communication system that will help him/her to understand – especially sand-timers or alarm clocks to convey time. This is especially so when it comes to activity rewards, since if the reward is to be successful it must be highly motivating for the learner and you don't want to be battling with him/her to get him/her off the computer when his/her 5 minutes' reward is up. Tell learners what's going to happen to them before it happens, and count down the activity ending – you've got 2 minutes left; you've got 1 minute left; you've got 20 seconds left; you've got 10 seconds left; 10, 9, 8, 7 . . . Give learners time to process change (especially when it's a withdrawal of a reward) and then give them more time.

2   Staff must be consistent in their approach.

3   Involve the learner in his/her own programme as much as possible. This particularly applies to more able learners (those who are operating at around P8 to Level 1 and above of the National Curriculum) who can fully understand consequences and who possess the reasoning skills to work with you.

9 Ensure that all staff are aware of the agreed methods of working

> ### CASE STUDY
>
> Kabir is 12 years old and has a rare degenerative condition which has seen him move from mainstream primary, where he was of average ability and physically very active, to a special school inside three years. The degeneration has been intellectual as well as physical and the prognosis is that it will continue. He is now educated within a single class of mixed ability ranging from PMLD (P3) to higher-functioning, ambulant SLD (Level 1 of the National Curriculum) with the class team of one teacher and three TAs teaching the class of seven students the whole range of the National Curriculum. He has been at the school (and with the same adult team) for just under two years. Kabir has recently had to be confined to a wheelchair and is now doubly incontinent, although he can still eat and drink independently. He can no longer read or write with any accuracy and is currently operating at around P7/8. His verbal skills, both receptive and expressive, remain quite good. Within the last six months Kabir has started to display significant challenging behaviours, refusing to be cooperative, using quite violent language and lashing out at members of staff. These behaviours seemed to go quite dramatically against type, since Kabir has always been for the most part quiet, gentle and whilst finding concentration difficult, able to focus well, with understanding, for most of the time. Significantly, the behaviours occurred with much greater frequency when Kabir was with staff other than his regular team, were especially prevalent at lunchtimes and most extreme during toileting and personal-care sessions.
>
> Although the class team had initially noted that Kabir was showing signs of anxiety, frustration and occasionally aggression during periods of personal care, they had quietly resolved the worst elements by remaining calm, not challenging and allowing Kabir plenty of time to be as independent in his own personal care as possible. This had had implications in terms of time, since toileting took much longer, but the team had made allowances for that within their class timetable.
>
> The major problems occurred for the most part with staff who were not regularly working with Kabir, especially at lunchtimes when his own team were on their own breaks, and who had several students to toilet in a relatively short space of time.

Why?, Consistency, Positive, Reward, Control, Time, Success

Even a fairly superficial reading of Kabir's history would lead one to assume that the **Why?** relates to Kabir's totally understandable reaction to his own physical and intellectual degeneration. Here was a boy who was apparently perfectly 'normal' one minute and in a special school the next. This was only supposed to happen to other people, yet here it was, happening to him. Within our simplification of the reasons for why (into either *attention seeking* or *task avoidance*) we could allocate this to *task avoidance*, since during personal care Kabir's task was to be docile, compliant and allow adults to do it for him. That's what happens in changing areas when staff have other duties to perform and a schedule to stick to. But Kabir didn't want other people to wipe his bottom, he wanted to do it himself, he wanted to be as independent as he could and since he hadn't had a lifetime's worth of personal care – this was a new experience for him; one that he didn't like. His own adult team knew him well enough to work this out, but other staff who didn't know him so well understandably treated him like all the other students in the school and the **consistency** broke down. Kabir's violent reactions brought on a negative and wary response from staff who only knew him from lunchtimes, and since no-one had talked to them about the **positive**, **reward**, **control**, **time**, **success** cycle which had worked with Kabir with his regular staff, the negative cycle continued.

What can we learn from ensuring that all staff are aware of the agreed methods of working with Kabir?

Firstly, and fundamentally, when it comes to behavioural issues, the dissemination of information is really important. Challenging behaviour is not something that just happens when it's convenient, and there's no such thing as a behaviour that doesn't affect all the teachers and TAs in a school, all the workers in a respite centre, all the staff in a play centre or after-school club. When all staff are not informed of the agreed methods of working they will of course deal with it as best they can, which can often be not very 'best' at all! But even just informing may well not be sufficient. We have already seen that consistency of approach in the organisation is absolutely vital, and in Kabir's case, a basic right; but if staff do not know the learner very well, have a different perspective of him, have different relationships with him, their understanding of the 'agreed methods' is likely to be very different. The information necessary for the workings of a successful behaviour management plan is about **much** more than the actual plan itself. Staff not directly involved with him need to know all of the background information – or at least as much as they possibly can know. They need to be guided and supported probably much more than staff who work with him all the time, to make up for their intrinsic lack of knowledge. In these circumstances it's not just information that's really important, it's also meetings and support as well. This clearly places a strain on management's resources, but they are issues that need to be addressed if the outcome is to be successful.

Secondly, there must be regular reviews of the behaviour management programmes and it is absolutely essential that each version is dated.

Thirdly, it makes sense for schools, who are likely to be the driving forces behind behaviour management programmes, to ensure that other organisations (as well as parents of course) are kept informed.

10 Provide a written protocol which describes how to respond to each challenging behaviour

Without being totally prescriptive about this, it is best that certain principles are followed when writing a behaviour management programme and needless to say it is absolutely essential that they are written down! This issue is dealt with in Chapter 8 'Writing a behaviour management programme'.

Summary

This chapter has reaffirmed both the defining characteristics of severe learning difficulties and the strength of the link between the learning difficulty and the challenging behaviour(s). I have listed ten tried-and-tested **strategies** for dealing with the many problems associated with challenging behaviour and severe learning difficulties, and in doing so I have borrowed heavily from previous work by John Harris (1995) and Harris *et al.* (1996). There is, after all, no point in reinventing something that's already been invented and is working perfectly well. All of the case studies related here have been actual cases known to me and all the strategies listed derive from the practical experience of a large group of SLD schools.

I have tried to tie in Harris's strategies to 'The Magnificent Seven' principles, but only because I have found that keeping the issues of **Why?**, **Consistency**, **Positive**, **Reward**, **Control**, **Time** and **Success** constantly in mind as a checklist to tick off in **every** case, irrespective of the strategy used, ensures that all of the main areas are covered.

These strategies are not mutually exclusive and you may wish to use more than one for the same issue – help the learner to establish positive relationships with one adult **and** introduce planned activities matched to the learner's strengths and weaknesses, for example. Some will clearly apply to every case – focusing on teaching language and communication; encouraging language and communication for meeting individual needs in everyday settings; conveying staff expectations clearly and providing consistent feedback; ensuring that all staff are aware of the agreed methods of working; providing a written protocol which describes how to respond to each challenging behaviour.

The strategies noted are not, of course, the only strategies that you might employ and there might be other equally effective courses to take, but it is an important point that none of those listed here involves punishment, aversive methods or restraint.

Notes

1 See Chapter 7 'Challenging behaviour and autistic spectrum disorders' for a more detailed discussion on sensory integration.

Challenging behaviour and profound and multiple learning difficulties

The long-term approach – part one

Throughout this chapter, I am going to talk in terms of the education and teaching of children, young people and adults with profound and multiple learning difficulties. This does not mean that the chapter is irrelevant for those of you such as parents, therapists, social workers, care and respite workers, etc., who might not consider yourselves to be formally involved in the educational process. It is clear that the learning difficulties for people with PMLD are so extreme (especially if they have additional challenging behaviours) that effective education must be multi-dimensional and regarded as being for life. It is not sufficient to expect formal education to cease at 19, 29 or 39 since learning is an extremely difficult and problematic business for someone with PMLD which will take many, many years – all of their lives in fact.

There are, equally, very strong arguments for considering this to also be the case for those with SLD. As any parent will tell you, however, it is undoubtedly true that establishments that are both willing and able to provide continued educational opportunities to a high standard beyond the age of 19 are very few and far between. Certainly local initiatives are being taken by some FE colleges and residential establishments, but generally speaking the national picture is bleak. I do not believe, however, that the funding (either centrally or locally) is lacking, merely that the funding is not guided towards providing high-quality lifelong learning. Whilst there has been a considerable drive towards higher education by the current government, we as a society are still stuck in the mainstream educational model that dictates that education ceases by the early twenties at the latest and that adults then turn to 'adult' things like going to work. That of course is neither possible not appropriate for people with PMLD and governments really do need to address the issue of directing existing 'care' funding into future 'educational' funding that is both of a high quality and rigorously inspected to Ofsted standards.

This chapter is also laid out somewhat differently from the last, in that my key point is that **the process of forming strong and mutually enjoyable relationships with children, young people and adults with PMLD is the only effective and lasting solution to challenging behaviours**. The case studies that I have experience of all point to the same 'solution', and whilst short-term remedies may be tried, these are unlikely to be effective without the relationships issue being addressed.

The long-term approach – part two

In Chapter 2 'What are SLD and PMLD?', I defined someone with profound learning difficulties as functioning at an intellectual level equivalent to a conventionally developing child of less than 18 months, and usually considerably less than 18 months. In behavioural terms, the key defining characteristics involve being pre-verbal in terms of intent; having no formal means of communication; being unable to independently imitate actions, sounds and movements; being totally physically reliant on others for all basic care and safety; having numerous sensory difficulties largely around developmental inabilities to integrate sensory stimulation; being totally unable to conceptualise abstract concepts; and having limited contingency awareness and an unrefined sense of cause and effect.

In educational terms, these key characteristics make teaching PMLD learners extremely difficult. Those of us who are familiar with PMLD can probably all remember our first introduction. Mine was in a post-16 group where I had been (deliberately) sheltered from the challenges of PMLD teaching, but since the Head of Post-16 had to attend a particularly important meeting, I had to teach the PMLD group. (I have to point out here that I had come into SLD teaching from moderate learning difficulties and my formal training had yet to start).

> '*What do you want me to do?*' I asked, somewhat naively.
>
> '*Well*', she replied, '*we're down for safety in the home. Why don't you do something around that?*'
>
> '*OK. No problem.*' – note the confidence!

I duly prepared what I thought was a sound lesson built around the dangers of fire – especially for the potential smokers among them – and started off the lesson by presenting my three PMLD students with a box of matches.

I'm not sure that I need to go on! Suffice it to say that I was 10 seconds in to a lesson that was supposed to last for an hour!

The long-term approach – part three

Paradoxically, however, whilst teaching children, young people and adults with PMLD is so very difficult and is probably the most intellectually challenging teaching I have ever done – you really do have to work incredibly hard to find 'ways into' some PMLD learners – the issue of challenging behaviours is relatively easily dealt with, for two main reasons. Firstly, the very act of good PMLD teaching – especially through the use of interactive approaches (which will be explored in more depth later in this chapter) is in itself an excellent and effective long-term strategy. Secondly, the long-term strategy really is the only positive option open to us. With SLD, all of the short-term strategies rely on the learner being able to make a connection between the behaviour and the desired learned response, but PMLD learners have by definition, limited contingency awareness and an unrefined sense of cause and effect. This automatically precludes the use of any behaviourist methods of changing behaviour, because behaviourism (in the form of operant conditioning at least) depends on a reasonably refined understanding of cause and effect.

I don't wish to spend a great deal of time discussing behaviourism because if you're interested there is a great deal of literature around. For those seeking the originals have a look at B. F. Skinner – especially Skinner (1953); for current research see the *Journal for the Experimental Analysis of Behavior* (JEAB) and the *Journal of Applied Behavior Analysis*, both American as you can tell from the spelling of behaviour; and for an extremely accessible but well-researched overview see James Atherton's excellent website at www.learningandteaching.info/learning/behaviour

Suffice it to say that Skinner's basic idea – that behaviour followed by some desirable or pleasurable consequence is more likely to recur (and similarly, behaviour followed by some undesirable consequences is less likely to recur) – follows on from work done by other behavioural scientists such as Pavlov, Watson and Thorndike. At its most basic, parents use behaviourist approaches all the time, as in 'If you behave yourself while we're in the supermarket you can have a sweetie at the checkout.' This is a classic case of operant conditioning using Stimulus–Response (S–R) with a Reinforcer, where the stimulus is the supermarket, the response is the good behaviour and the reinforcer (the reward) is the sweetie. Similarly 'If you muck about in the supermarket you'll get a clip round the ear 'ole' is a classic case of operant conditioning using aversive strategies; but as we're not using punishment or negative techniques, we won't go there!

Behaviourism is, however, also a learning theory and has been much used in the past by educationalists for teaching skills to pupils with both SLD and PMLD. Before its demise, the Inner London Education Authority (ILEA) produced a huge ring-bound folder entitled *Cumulative Records* which 'helpfully' broke down every conceivable task into tiny bite-sized chunks. If you wanted to teach someone to eat independently you used a behaviourist 'chaining' technique whereby you:

1   taught him/her how to hold a spoon;
2   taught him/her how to hold a spoon for 3 seconds;
3   taught him/her how to hold a spoon for 10 seconds;
4   taught him/her how to load the spoon;
5   taught him/her how to bring the spoon to his/her mouth;
6   taught him/her how to put the spoon into her his/mouth;
7   taught him/her how to take the spoon out of his/her mouth, etc., etc.

And eventually you put all of the individual 'links' together to form the chain.

While being very circumspect about the use of behaviourist methods with those with profound learning difficulties, Collis and Lacey (1996) do nonetheless point out that they can usefully be used in the form of reflex conditioning – as opposed to the more sophisticated operant conditioning – in, for example:

1   developing self-help skills, such as holding a spoon;
2   where learning is important without necessarily having to understand why – fire will burn;

3 the acquisition of essential rote skills, such as pressing a switch or standing on the count of three, etc.

The key point here is that these are examples of reflex conditioning, where the understanding of the individual is neither here nor there, and the ability of the learner to process the lesson is not taken into account. Nonetheless, reflex conditioning can play a major part in short-term solutions to some challenging behaviours.

CASE STUDY

Michael is 11 years old, has cerebral palsy and PMLD (functioning between P2 and P3) and has just come to the secondary SLD school from the primary SLD school in the same LEA. His notes show that he has always bitten when he doesn't want to do something – especially being put in his standing frame – but since attending the secondary school he is now biting for no apparent reason. To make it worse, he seems to find this very funny, laughing uproariously every time he does it, especially when it's really painful. Although Mum says she's noticed it at home, it's a new behaviour and she's blaming the school!

What can we learn from this?

We have already established that there's no such thing as a behaviour without a reason, even though the reason might not be apparent or make any sense to us. The reason for this particular behaviour starting up in the first place was almost impossible to fathom other than Michael stumbling on it (or rather biting on it) by chance, and getting a big kick out of the response he received from the bitten adult. If that is so, the laughter is not a callous enjoyment of others' suffering, but an enjoyment in the reaction of the individual being bitten. Remember that people with profound learning difficulties are very unlikely to have a refined sense of empathy for others, and their delight in the extreme facial expressions, cries, shouts, screams, etc. of the bitten may well be as a small baby might experience. It is probably all much like a pantomime, with the bitten person being the clown!

We therefore need to work on both a short and long-term solution. In the short term, if we are aware that he is likely to bite when flesh gets too close, we can gently deflect his mouth away (possibly turning the intended bite into a kiss) but giving him the same sort of extreme reaction he got from a bite. Much as we might for a very small baby, widening our eyes and mouths in a look of feigned surprise when Michael gives a kiss on our arm, and generally playing the clown for him, may well give him the same buzz as the unacceptable bite. The persistent and consistent use of this deflection tactic can be classified as reflex conditioning. If we do it often enough we will hopefully (i) teach Michael that this is the appropriate (and enjoyable) thing to do and (ii) extinguish the challenging behaviour by **teaching him** to forget the biting. The less he bites, the less he gets the reaction and the less it is reinforced.

Michael bites because he enjoys the reaction, which in many ways is merely an extension of attention seeking. As with all attention-seeking behaviours with those with severe and profound learning difficulties, the only long-term solution is to give the attention. Clearly, however, we cannot (must not!) give the attention when he bites, rather we must teach a better way of gaining satisfaction from attention. In other words we must teach Michael a better way of communicating and the very best way to do that is through Intensive Interaction. These may well be *famous last words* but in all of the times that I have had 'up-close and personal' Intensive Interactions with children, young people and adults who have displayed extremes of violent behaviour, I can honestly say that I have never been injured as a result. That is not to say that I have never been injured, just not during Intensive Interaction sessions. Perhaps this is because the point of the sessions is to have fun, reflect the learners' moods, adopt gentle teaching practices, etc., which do not in themselves challenge the learners.

With PMLD as much as SLD, it is equally important in behavioural teaching that in the long term, **the learner has to want to change** if strategies are to be successful. We may adopt short-term reflex-conditioning strategies to overcome specific immediate difficulties like Michael's biting, but Michael still has to be included in working out a better long-term resolution. This means that the learner has to be an active part of the learning process rather than a passive part, and that the behavioural teaching must not merely be done **to** the child, it must be done **with** the child. It is therefore self evident that the process of teaching – the way that we actually teach, the foundations of our relationships with the child – is the key to changing the behaviour.

In behavioural terms, it is not what we teach children, young people and adults with PMLD that matters, it's how we teach them.

Why?

Trying to understand the reasons behind displays of challenging behaviour in someone who is pre-verbal and has no formal communication system at all, who may or may not even make eye contact and who may or may not give a recognisable and consistent indication that something is wrong, is not necessarily easy. We are likely to be largely into the realms of guesswork, though this can be an educated guess in the same way as a mother can guess why her 3-month-old baby is crying. Usually this is a simple process of (i) elimination – she can't be hungry because I've just fed her; she can't be wet because I've just changed her (ii) context – she can't be teething because she's too young and (iii) previous experience – it might be colic because she's been having quite bad bouts recently. Clearly knowledge is all, and the better you know your learner the more educated your guesses will be.

Part of that knowledge will naturally be related to specific conditions and syndromes, though it's probably true to say that there are very few conditions related to profound learning difficulties that are specifically responsible for challenging behaviour. Lesch-Nyhan and Cornelia de Lange spring to mind – both involving compulsion towards self-injurious behaviours such as extreme skin picking – but there are few (if any) others.

More commonplace conditions which are much more likely to be influential are:

Table 6.1 Conditions likely to affect challenging behaviour in children, young people and adults with PMLD

Diet	Cramp	Anxiety
Discomfort	Drug side effects	Sexual frustration
Hunger	Epilepsy	Stress
Illness	Itching and general skin irritation	Uncertainty
Pain	Periods	
Thirst	Reflux	
Tiredness	Sleep problems	
	Swallowing difficulties	

and I'm sure you could add to this list with a little bit of thought.

With anybody with PMLD who displays challenging behaviour it is therefore always worthwhile to go through a checklist like the one noted above to discount the obvious before embarking on any more radical programmes, since we need to decide if the behaviour is health related or a learned response. It is, of course, true that a number (or even all) of the above may cause a learned response if the issues are not dealt with and it is still important to remember that the **learning difficulty itself is the key factor in the continued existence of the challenging behaviour**.

With PMLD especially, however, there are a number of additional factors which may lead to a learned response. These will include:

1 communication difficulties – an even more relevant factor than with SLD since there will be no formal expressive communication system owned by the individual and there is often no way of being absolutely sure how good their receptive language (their understanding of language) or other communicative forms are;

2 attempts to exercise control over situations and other people, usually in a negative way;

3 distress – perhaps due to anxiety, environmental uncertainty, sensory overload, a failure to treat a specific medical condition, etc.;

4 boredom – not being able to exercise control over the vast majority of their external environment may well lead to an increased tendency to exercise control over themselves. This will in turn lead to self-stimulatory and stereotypical behaviours such as eye poking, hand biting, rocking, etc.;

5 the addictive qualities of self-inflicted pain means that self-injurious behaviours are often extremely difficult to extinguish. Here the body 'self administers' endogenous opiates – the beta endorphines that the body produces naturally with pain – a procedure often associated with the 'high'

experienced by those of you with well-tuned athletic bodies who attend gyms regularly. It is also commonly associated with masochism and sexual gratification and can clearly exercise a considerable hold.

Generally, self-injurious behaviours (SIB) are relatively common in those with PMLD, and even though most are at the fairly low level of hand biting and eye poking, these can get to be serious issues if the hand gets festered or the eyeball is poked out completely!

CASE STUDY

Toni was two when she came to the school, and she was already crying. I don't mean crying for a few minutes, or even a few hours. Sometimes she didn't cry just for a few days, because this cry might last for weeks (and weeks . . . and weeks!). And not only were there cries there were also self-injurious behaviours such as hand bites, banging her head and slapping her face. She would pull others' hair and scratch them, often digging her nails into the flesh in her anxiety and stress. Nor did this behaviour diminish over time, but carried on well into her teens. And the reason? Who knew then and who knows now? Toni's mother, who remained sane despite the lack of sleep, tried just about everything anyone could think of – and when she'd run out of logical reasons, she naturally tried every other theory that was about at the time. No cause, either physical or psychological, was ever discovered.

Of course we tried Intensive Interaction, and whilst it definitely helped while the Interaction was taking place, Toni's distress was so great that there was no carry over, in the sense that the relaxing effects of the Interaction lasted sometimes for no longer than a few minutes. There were calm times, which often lasted several weeks at a time, but these were unpredictable and seemed to occur at home far more frequently than at school. This in turn would seem to imply that the general hustle and bustle and sensory overload of the SLD school was at fault, and indeed it may well have been that had we had our time with Toni over again, we would do things differently, especially with regard to protecting her from sensory over-stimulation.

In this instance, however, the only long-lasting remedy was in the form of medication which despite causing Toni to put on a considerable amount of weight did manage to calm her for lengthy periods. Let me make it absolutely clear that I am most definitely not in favour of medication as a 'cure' for challenging behaviour – the almost universal use of drugs such as Ritalin for ADHD diagnosis is long overdue serious questioning – but occasionally (*very* occasionally) it may be the only answer. We should therefore not rule it out totally. We must, however, continue to be very sceptical and look upon medication as a *last* resort when all other options have been tried. Rightly, Toni's mother resisted the drug option until Toni was well into her teens, and indeed has continued to be wary of it up to the present time.

This case study is therefore saying nothing more than we must continue to hold an open mind to all options, as long as they're positive and in the very best interests of the child, young person or adult who is presenting the challenging behaviour. One of those options **may** be medication but only as a last resort when **everything** imaginable has been tried . . . and **everything** imaginable has failed!

What can we learn from this?

Once again, it is really important that we don't get overwhelmed with either the difficulties of assessing the causes of the behaviour or the multiplicity of behaviours displayed. Once we rule out the *other factors* of pain, illness, hunger, thirst, etc. noted above, it is still possible to deal with issues of challenging behaviour by simplifying the **Why?** and reverting to the two over-arching causes of attention seeking or task avoidance.

Attention seeking

It may be that numerous behaviours in children, young people and adults with PMLD have attention seeking as the root cause, but it will undoubtedly be very different from the 'knowing' attention seeking of the SLD child and indeed it may be very hard to recognise it as attention seeking at all. The person with SLD who is demanding your attention will make it very clear – they'll be in your face; make sure you're watching before they exhibit the behaviour; be very aware of your presence and your reaction; be invariably prepared to accept a negative response (such as telling off) as being better than no response at all. The person with PMLD, on the other hand, might well exhibit the behaviour whether you're watching or not, indeed they might well exhibit the behaviour whether you're in the room or not! If it seems a bit bizarre to suggest that someone might be attention seeking in an empty room, it is only bizarre if that person has a refined understanding of cause and effect. In other words, it may be that because the person **needs** attention they exhibit the behaviours, because the behaviours are an extension of their frustration and because they have not made the connection between needing attention and the ability of other people to provide that attention through human contact. Most people with PMLD are essentially passive communicators (Ware 2003), who will often respond to a communication but will never initiate one. Only the higher functioning – those operating developmentally around 18 months who will have many of the learning characteristics of the person with SLD – will be able to make the connection and be able to communicate declaratively (Bates *et al.* 1975, Park 1998), that is, declare without prompt, their desire to communicate. By definition, this is extremely rare in people with PMLD.

Task avoidance

Here, it is much easier to make the connection and a number of the case studies at the end of this chapter have task avoidance at their core. Not surprisingly for people with PMLD who almost without exception have absolutely no opportunities to exercise any control over their lives at any time, in any place, with any one, desperate remedies are occasionally (and sometimes very often) reached for. If you can't control your life to make nice things happen to you, you may at least be able to stop the bad things happening to you, even if the bad thing is something as essential as physiotherapy or learning how to hold a spoon.

There are two issues here.

Knowing about the learning needs of the individual

Firstly, as with those with ASD in the following chapter, a considerable number of problems can be simply overcome by making sure that our practice meets the learning needs of the individual. It is indeed quite remarkable how many of the strategies overlap for PMLD and ASD. We can for example:

1   Try and give as much information as possible to individuals using non-linguistic means by using such strategies as objects of reference (Ockelford 2002), signing, touch cues, musical cues (as in playing the same piece of music every week before art and a different piece of music every week before sensory story, etc.) and maybe even familiar photographs or symbols for the higher functioning.

2   We can keep routines the same – always count to three before physically moving someone, always go to the toilet at the same times in the day.

3   We can try and ensure that only familiar staff work with them, and always for the same sessions as far as possible.

4   We can use as little language as possible and focus our language when we have to use it, as in 'Michael . . . here is a red ball . . . a red ball' rather than 'Right Michael, look what we've got for you. A wonderful, bright, shiny red ball. What are you going to do with that Michael? Would you like to roll it to Stephanie? Or perhaps Louise? What do think Michael? Eh Michael? Eh? Come on slowcoach, roll the ball . . .'

5   We can try and ensure that there is as little sensory confusion as possible by just working down one sensory channel at a time. Don't speak when there's music playing; don't have music on in the background when you're trying to work; make sure the temperature and light is constant; don't talk across or over the children; don't put sugar into white mixing bowls or raisins into dark ones; conduct regular sensory inventories to make sure that sensory confusions don't arise.

6   Give the children time, more time and then more time. Don't expect a lesson to last one lesson – it will have to be repeated several times.

These are all standard good practice for working with people with PMLD and will already be fairly familiar. There are I'm sure others that are equally valid and it is not meant to be an exhaustive list. The point is that we cannot expect people with PMLD to concentrate on us if we don't concentrate on them. If people are not in control of their own lives, we have to make as much of their lives as predictable – and therefore as stress, anxiety and uncertainty free – as possible.

Knowing about your own power

Secondly, we cannot expect children, young people and adults with PMLD to give up their exercise of power through the use of challenging behaviours, if we're not prepared to have relationships with them that are not based on our overwhelming control. We must be prepared to have as the base a relationship that's founded on equality, trust, friendship and reciprocity. We must be prepared to enter into a relationship that's based on love.

CASE STUDY

Fred is 8 years old, has profound learning difficulties and is functioning at around P3. He is ambulant, quite active and lives alone with his mother, although she occasionally receives some help from her brother. Despite the fact that Fred has always had a bit of a passion for water (he loved swimming and would play for ages with a running tap) he has started to refuse to have anything to do with water. He is quite a strong boy and digs his nails into the flesh of anyone who tries to wash him and as a result his mother is covered in scars. Fred is starting to smell very badly and his groin area is covered in sores from his pad.

What can we learn from this?

It may well be that something has caused Fred to be frightened of water, and though we never found out, we could make educated guesses – for example, somebody forcing him to wash when the sores first appeared. You may never find out what causes the behaviour to start, but if we refer back to the two likely causes and file this under task avoidance, it may help to make a little more sense of the issues involved. Like all task-avoidance problems, we have to ensure success, and ensure it slowly; and we have to give control back to the learner. In this instance, though Fred needs to be cleaned, this does not have to mean water and can equally well be achieved with wet wipes, but it might still mean several days of dabbing around the infected area before you can get to the sore bits. Fred can then also be slowly reintroduced to water, through lots of water games, etc., and trust that we're not going to hurt him.

Once again, the key point is that it is our relationship with those with PMLD which is at the core of the behaviour and only by addressing this relationship can we hope to address the behaviour.

Gentle teaching

As a result of what they and their colleagues considered to be an excessive reliance on skills-based teaching and behaviourist methods of working, John McGee and Frank Menolascino wrote:

> all humans long for meaning, companionship, choice and freedom. For those who are marginalised, this search is more laborious . . . and choice becomes a hollow sound in a world of behavior modification. Some say that skill acquisition and compliance are the most fundamentally necessary elements in family and community life . . . but these elements are not the cornerstones of the human condition.
>
> (McGee and Menolascino 1991, p. 75)

McGee and Menolascino argued that friendship, trust, bonding and, indeed, love **need to be taught** and that only by giving everyone the opportunity of having

meaningful human relationships can we ask them to give up potentially destructive behaviours.

CASE STUDY

Naomi was only 13 when she died. She had severe quadriplegia (lack of use of all four limbs), very high muscle tone (her arms were, for example, constantly tucked into her chin with her fists closed tight), coupled with very poor head and neck control. She was often very ill and when in school seemed to spend most of her time asleep. Some questioned whether her tendency to sleep was deliberate, since she would often close her eyes when approached by an adult intent on getting her to do something. She fitted often at the slightest noise and was incredibly difficult to engage.

Did Naomi have challenging behaviour?

What can we learn from this?

What a difficult question that is! But going back to original definitions of challenging behaviour it would appear that of the 11 precepts posited by O'Brien (1998), 8 directly applied to Naomi if we take her sleeping and lack of engagement as deliberate.

- *The behaviour prevents the child from participating in the curriculum.*
- *The behaviour is not considered appropriate to the child's age and level of development.*
- *The behaviour results in the child being continually isolated from their peers.*
- *The behaviour has a negative impact upon the child's independence.*
- *The behaviour is placing extreme threats or demands on individual staff, staff teams or school resources.*
- *The behaviour reinforces the child's negative self-concept and low self-esteem.*
- *The behaviour is restricting the opportunities for a child to develop new skills.*
- *The behaviour is creating a dangerous environment for the child, for other children and for adults. This would include self-injurious behaviour.*

(pp. 71–2)

Clearly behaviours which allow the person to switch off can be severely challenging – I also knew a boy who deliberately fitted whenever anyone suggested working and especially when anyone brought a standing frame into the room! Though we have to be careful with some very profoundly disabled persons, in that just staying alive is challenge enough never mind working as well, there are certainly going to be a few who task avoid by falling asleep, turning away, keeping very quiet, bringing on seizures, etc. But again, with all task-avoiding behaviours, we need to make sure of (i) success and (ii) finding ways to give control back to the learner and again these are best achieved by ensuring that the learner **is actually able** to enter into relationships. Because we are constantly making demands on the learner (to work, to extend themselves, to learn or, perhaps, in their terms, to experience discomfort, to experience pain, to experience uncertainty) the relationship is bound to be one of distrust. The learner has to believe that they can take real value from relationships. This has to encompass an **equality** within the relationship rather than a dominance of the teacher over the pupil, the adult over the child, the able over the disabled.

Jean Ware (2003) has noted that babies and infants with PMLD are likely to have interactions with their caregivers in which:

1   they are the passive partners;

2   they get comparatively few responses from their caregivers;

3   the caregiver is the dominant partner;

4   there are often clashes between the infant and the caregiver (such as when both are 'speaking' at once).

In other words relationships with people with PMLD are framed by the control being almost totally given over to the teacher/carer/parent/therapist.

CASE STUDY

Fatima originally came to the school aged nine. As far as we were able to discern, she had not had any recognisable schooling until then. Fatima was fairly high-functioning PMLD, probably operating at the intellectual equivalent of a 12 to 15-month-old (P3/4); she was ambulant, determined and very anti-social. She would quite happily stay in a class as long as she was able to sit on her own, holding a dolly, balloon or teddy, rocking back and forth and singing quietly to herself.

Whenever we tried to engage her she would react quite violently, often hitting women in their breasts and men in their groin. Clearly a girl of discernment! She would hit with a closed fist and it could hurt quite a lot. She refused to sit next to anybody (staff or pupil) and would lash out sideways, again with a closed fist, if she felt anyone was too close. She would often have *major* temper tantrums, when all hell would break loose with objects and fists and screams flying everywhere at once. Clearly, we were going to be unable to even start to get involved with skills-based teaching (or any other teaching for that matter) whilst Fatima flatly refused to engage and got so angry when we tried. We therefore embarked on a programme of Intensive Interaction.

The first thing to do was to try and get close to her, so we devised a strategy of one person approaching her from the front, slowly and at her level (standing if she was, on the floor if she was, sitting if she was). We used no language other than 'Hello Fatima' as an introduction and gently took her hand, rolled the hand over so that the palm was facing up and stroked her palm until she pulled her hand away – which initially would, of course, be after only a second or two. Fatima would often hit out at these times, and it was then a matter of catching her hand before rolling it flat to stroke and hoping she didn't hit you with the other hand! We would do this several times a day, initially for only a couple of minutes, but soon for longer, so that after a year, Fatima was getting around two or three (formal) Intensive Interaction sessions a day lasting for about 20 minutes each.

After 18 months or so, Fatima suddenly, without any warning, looked one of the staff in the eye and held out her hand, palm upwards towards the person. Trumpets blew and tears rolled because *Hallelujah*, Fatima had independently communicated and was now actively involved in the Interaction rather than just being a passive receiver! From that point on she continued to use this as an indication that she wanted to 'talk'.

But we wanted to move her on further, and thought that we might be able to develop her vocalisations – she continued to 'sing' to herself when self-engaging. Now, as well as using the hand out method, we introduced the 'raspberry' game. This involved blowing a gentle raspberry on her neck after indicating this was going to happen by making a soft, long, whooping noise rising in scale from low to high – an approximation of the sounds she made to herself. Again, 18 months or so passed by and again, Fatima suddenly looked at one of her favourite people from across the room and went 'wwwwhhhoooooooooooop'!! Now not only was Fatima openly communicating her desire for a 'chat', but was vocalising to do it!

By the time Fatima left school at 19, one of her main Intensive Interaction targets was to let people go after 15 minutes or so of working, rather than hanging on to them for dear life!

What can we learn from this?

There are a few, very important points that arise from this.

1   This is not a book about Intensive Interaction. If you haven't already done so, *please* read Nind and Hewett (2001) *A Practical Guide to Intensive Interaction*. They have written lots of books on the subject, but this is the easiest to read and the most accessible, with loads of relevant case studies. If you're interested in first-hand accounts of Intensive Interaction try and hear either Melanie Nind or Dave Hewett (or both if you can) speak, either at a conference or get them into your school for an INSET. They're very good and it's well worth the money!

2   This is not an isolated case. **Intensive Interaction really does work**.

3   Just reading Fatima's case study seems to imply that she moved from horror child to wonder child in just three years. Unfortunately this was not so! Fatima continued to have mega tantrums, to stamp and scream and occasionally hit out at anyone within striking distance, and continued right up until she left school – and, I must assume, beyond – but we learnt that this was a natural part of her character. When she first came, we were always trying to work out why she was behaving in the way that she was. Was she hungry, thirsty, wet, tired? Was she ill? Was there a regular monthly cycle to her moods? Were there certain lessons, or people that she took exception to? What we learnt was that, more than anything, Fatima had an extremely feisty personality. If something upset her she was going to let you and the whole world know about it . . . bigtime. Intensive Interaction allowed us to get beyond the learning difficulty to really know the person that Fatima was, as

only a friend can know a friend. And the big bonus was that when Fatima did lose it, Intensive Interaction calmed her almost immediately.

What Intensive Interaction is doing is teaching people with PMLD about the fundamentals of communication. According to Nind and Hewett (2001) these are:

- use and understanding of eye contact;
- use of facial expression;
- learning to 'read' facial expression;
- learning to enjoy giving attention to another person;
- taking turns in exchanges of behaviour;
- use and understanding of physical contact;
- use and understanding of gestures;
- learning to 'read' body language;
- learning about personal space;
- learning to concentrate and attend.

Further, there is a very strong and persuasive argument that suggests that the principles of an Interactive approach are ones that should be fundamental to all good PMLD teaching (Collis and Lacey 1996) – and some might argue teaching *per se*. These principles are that:

- *learning is dependent upon good interpersonal relationships;*
- *there is sensitivity to feedback from the learner;*
- *the focus is on understanding rather than skill acquisition;*
- *the emphasis is on respect, negotiation, participation and positive regard. The student's contribution is valued and positively built upon;*
- *it is a process-based approach, in which the quality of the teaching and learning is as important as the achievement of objectives – indeed **the quality of the process becomes (one of) the major objectives**;*
- *teaching is not always dependent on dividing that which is to be taught into its constituent parts;*
- *it is based on intrinsic motivation, rather than extrinsic rewards – that is, the reward is in the pleasure to be gained from the process;*
- *it is not the learner who fails to learn, but the teacher who fails to provide an adequate learning opportunity.*

pp. 13 (my emphasis)

Autism and PMLD

There is no doubt in my mind that autism and profound learning difficulties can and do occasionally exist side by side. It is, however, by no means easy to be accurate in such a diagnosis and as I have discussed in relation to potential ASD/SLD dual diagnosis, we need to be cautious in assuming that the existence of certain behaviours equates to autism. Extreme communication problems, difficulties in social interaction and sensory confusions are, by definition, common features of all PMLD and these coupled with a tendency towards stereotypical, repetitive and obsessional behaviours may well lead the unwary towards a dual ASD/PMLD diagnosis. If you are certain, however, (and it must be a big 'if') the autism must take precedence when dealing with challenging behaviour and I would refer you to Chapter 7 'Challenging behaviour and autistic spectrum disorders'.

Having spent the last several pages of this chapter dealing in some detail with **Why?** I would like to cover the other six of 'The Magnificent Seven' principles of challenging behaviour fairly briefly. This is because **Consistency**, **Positive**, **Reward**, **Control**, **Time** and **Success** all follow on logically from placing Intensive Interaction, and Interactive techniques of working with children, young people and adults with PMLD, at the heart of your relationships with them.

Consistency

The important element of consistency here is that the *gentle teaching* approach that underpins all Interactive techniques is used by everyone who comes into contact with the person from your organisation. Having said that, each individual will of course have a quite different relationship with the person, because they will know the person as only they can, but each will be based on friendship, trust and a deep bonding between the two.

Positive

It logically follows that if the relationship is one of friendship, trust and a deep bonding, it must be positive. There is no room for aversive or negative techniques that automatically demand that the teacher, worker, carer or parent adopts a position of power over the person with PMLD.

Reward

The reward is intrinsic and is in the actual process of the friendship, trust and bonding that develops between the two participants of the Interactive process. It is incredibly strong and incredibly powerful. It liberates the relationship from the deep constraints of the learning difficulty and overcomes the problems of understanding cause and effect that afflict all with PMLD.

Control

More than anything, Intensive Interaction allows the learner to take control. It allows them to experience deep and meaningful relationships that do not have language as their base, do not demand a high-functioning understanding of the nuances of body language, facial expression, context and history. Constant repetition allows the learner to take these relationships into other areas of learning, which in turn eases the learning process itself. It gives them the confidence to explore the world around them with people they know and trust and love.

Time

Intensive Interaction and Interactive techniques teach **us** about time scales. With PMLD, there are very few short-term solutions and there are likely to be many reversals along the way. But we're in for the long haul and we learn that the overall trend is for improvement, even though this may take **many** years to achieve.

Success

Children, young people and adults with PMLD need to achieve as much as anybody and of course they need to recognise when they have been successful. Giving rewards of any description as a direct and immediate indication of success is fraught with difficulties for those who are unable to make the connection between cause and effect. Without contingency awareness there can be no real understanding of the link between behaviour and reward or punishment. Those who have learned to avoid human bonding and who cannot appreciate the value of social interaction as a reward, are never going to understand or appreciate the link in any meaningful way. Success, therefore, has to be based on the ability of the relationships formed to convey achievement through non-verbal means; through the uses of friendship, trust, bonding and love.

Summary

This chapter has detailed the defining characteristics of profound and multiple learning difficulties as they apply to those expressing challenging behaviours. Although the teaching of those with PMLD is extremely complex, the issue of behavioural challenges is less so, because so many of the strategies that we might use with the more academically or intellectually able are denied to us. Since children, young people and adults with PMLD do not have a refined sense of cause and effect, the behaviourist strategy of rewarding positive behaviours is not open to us, because the person with PMLD would not be able to make the essential connection between the new behaviour and the reward. We therefore have to look for alternative short and long-term strategies.

Short-term strategies will probably involve *deflection* techniques – catching a slap and turning it into a stroke; diverting a bite into a kiss – so that the learner no longer associates the challenging behaviour with whatever the response was. The essential thing here is to **extinguish** the behaviour through lack of use, so that the learner *forgets* over a period of time.

Short-term strategies are, however, pointless if we are unable to develop relationships with the PMLD learner which go beyond the fact that it is **we** who are in control. For somebody with PMLD, relationships will always be unequal. **We** decide when to engage; **we** decide how long to engage for; **we** decide on what terms to engage; **we** decide what to engage about; **we** decide when the engagement finishes. The relationship is entirely unequal, because **we** are in total control.

Long-term relationships with children, young people and adults with PMLD must be based on a more equal footing if they are to be positive and effective.

The very best way of doing that is through **Intensive Interaction** techniques as propounded by Melanie Nind and Dave Hewett, because these are the only bases for a relationship where the PMLD learner has some control over the outcome. Interactive approaches to learning are based on a **process** approach, in which the quality of the teaching and learning is as important as the achievement of objectives. Indeed **the quality of the process *becomes* the objective**. It is therefore not the learner who fails to learn, but the teacher who fails to provide an adequate learning opportunity. Intensive Interaction does, however, provide a real opportunity for the learner to learn about the real value of relationships, and indeed the real value of being human.

Challenging behaviour and autistic spectrum disorders

In Chapter 3 'What is ASD?' we established that autism is a complex neurological condition affecting communication, social interaction and flexibility of thinking and behaviour – otherwise known as the Triad of Impairments. To these we might add the *fourth impairment* of sensory processing. The core features that make up the condition of autism are (i) durable over time and (ii) accompanied by rituals, compulsions, high levels of anxiety and a desire for sameness.

This chapter is concerned with those experiencing the dual diagnosis of autism and severe learning difficulties (ASD/SLD). It argues strongly that we cannot expect people with autism to learn (new and more acceptable behaviours) if we are not prepared to teach them in a way in which they are able to learn. We would not dream of teaching English people in Greek (or Greek people in English) without making any effort to translate, adjust, differentiate and generally account for the fact that there might be no understanding of the language used. Why would we want to teach autistic people in ways that take no account of their autism?

There are certain incontrovertible facts here – (i) there is (at the time of publication) no known cure for autism and (ii) it is not possible to take the condition away. There is not a pill to swallow or an operation to perform that can cut the autism out – autism is for life. As in the argument within both severe and profound learning difficulties therefore, the learning impairment is likely to be crucial in the formation and perpetuation of challenging behaviours. We have already established that it is impossible (and, indeed, potentially extremely harmful) to discount the learning difficulty and carry on as though it didn't exist. The difference with autism is, however, that irrespective of the degree of learning difficulty the existence of the autism becomes **the** crucial factor. The Triad of Impairments; Theory of Mind; problems with Central Coherence; Sensory Impairments; all exist to a greater or lesser degree in all those diagnosed with autism. These issues **must be addressed** when trying to arrive at successful strategies for dealing with challenging behaviour in those within the autistic spectrum. Of course the additional learning difficulties are meaningful, but it must not be expected that strategies suitable for those with SLD will automatically be successful for those with ASD, even if the person with autism also has severe learning difficulties. **The autism will always take precedence when deciding on possible strategies for altering behaviour.**

Accepting that there is no known cure for autism means accepting that it is impossible to expect the person with autism to act as though they didn't have autism – it would be like asking someone with PMLD to stop mucking about and take themselves down to the toilet **right now!** It's not the person with autism who has to make the initial change – **it's we who have to change.** This does not mean that we must accept the behaviours – people with autism have to live in the real world too – but **we must provide the conditions under which children, young people and adults with autism are able to learn,** *before* **we can expect changes in behaviour**. As Theo Peeters has pointed out:

> We need to adapt our teaching of meaning to (the autistic person's) brain functioning, instead of expecting them to adapt to our level of meaning. The strong should adapt to the weaker, not the other way round.
>
> (Peeters 2000, p. 16)

Again, as with SLD and PMLD, **changing behaviour is a learning process**.

There is a chapter on challenging behaviour in Rita Jordan's (2001) excellent book *Autism with Severe Learning Difficulties* and though it is not my intention to repeat that, I will occasionally refer back to it. If you are experiencing difficulties in this area with your ASD charges – whatever their ages – and are serious about tackling challenging behaviour, I would strongly urge you to read the whole book, but at least Chapter 10. I am therefore going to presume that you have, or are going to, read all or part of *Autism with Severe Learning Difficulties* as a very minimum.

You might also want to look at Clements and Zarkowska (2000) and Whitaker (2001), both well laid out and accessible (especially Whitaker).

As with SLD and PMLD, those children, young people and adults with the dual diagnosis of autism and severe learning difficulties will equally benefit from us taking account of 'The Magnificent Seven' of **Why?**, **Consistency**, **Positive**, **Reward**, **Control**, **Time**, **Success**.

Why?

The problem with **Why?** is essentially the problem with autism. The more you know about autism the more you will understand why. Unfortunately, autism itself is pretty complicated, needs considerable study (see Chapter 3 'What is ASD?' for a short but essential reading list) and, of course, each individual person with autism is likely to be different to a greater or lesser degree.

Also, as Jordan (2001) astutely notes, there is no such thing as an *autistic* behaviour – there are only things that people with autism **really enjoy** doing, or that are **really important** to them, or things they do when they are **really under stress**. If there is one thing that we must always hold in our minds it is that **autism is a condition of almost permanent stress** and our role is therefore, largely, to reduce that stress!

It is also clear when working with children, young people and adults with autism that it is not possible to merely fall back on the premise that the behaviour is likely to be either attention seeking or task avoidance. Of course these may well be issues, but other factors are often heavily to the fore, most notably: behaviours as communications; sensory issues; problems with transition and unplanned change; and panic, fears and phobias.

Challenging behaviour as a communication

The challenging behaviour of children, young people and adults with autism can often be regarded as being a basic communication. Sometimes this is a poor communication, sometimes this is awful communication, but it is communication nonetheless.

CASE STUDY

Tommy is 8 years old and has been diagnosed ASD/SLD. He is quite high functioning, operating academically at the equivalent of a conventionally developing 3 or 4-year-old – around P7. He can communicate verbally, though his language is often echolalic (repeating the last words spoken to him).

A new TA (Janet) has been brought into the class and they have struck up an immediate rapport. She is calm, doesn't go 'up' when Tommy gets overexcited and is quietly firm with him. Tommy works with her very well.

At lunchtimes, however, when Janet is on playground duty, Tommy has started to pinch her. The first time it happened, he was doing his usual walking around the playground, touching specific objects as he went. He then walked up to Janet and looked at her. She naturally said 'Hello Tommy' and he pinched her, quite hard on the fleshy part of her upper arm. Janet, knowing not to reward a negative behaviour, decided to ignore the pinch and Tommy walked away. But it happened again after a couple of minutes, and then again and now it is happening quite a lot of the time and to other members of staff, who are not all so ready to ignore. Clearly, staff don't like the behaviour (it hurts!) and it is very difficult to ignore; there is a natural tendency to 'tell off'; some are adopting the policy of saying 'Gentle hands' to Tommy; the principle of ignoring the behaviour doesn't seem to be working.

Why Tommy chose this particular time and place to pinch Janet might be extremely difficult to work out, but we can probably hazard a guess that this is a communication on Tommy's part. He was saying '*Hello*' to Janet. The fact that it was a very painful and unacceptable way of saying hello does not alter the fact of the behaviour being, to Tommy at least, a reasonable thing to do. It may be that this is something he did in the past (perhaps to his mother) and it was then very effective in gaining her attention. It would therefore be logical for Tommy to use it again to say 'Hello' to Janet, especially when she's not working directly with him in her general supervisory role in the playground. Although Janet is ignoring the behaviour, it is not important for Tommy to immediately gain her attention, since he is using it as a point of social contact, much as we might say 'Hello' to someone as we pass in the corridor without any expectation that the person will stop and talk to us. Having used it with Janet, it might seem logical for Tommy to use it with others. Now, however, he gets different reactions, interesting reactions, exciting reactions. Now the behaviour (the same behaviour) has a totally different function for Tommy – it provides entertainment!

There are three immediate points that arise from this behaviour. Firstly, it is both possible and can indeed be fairly commonplace to have the same behaviour serving different functions for a learner. Secondly, the principle of giving attention to an attention seeker still applies to those with ASD/SLD. Thirdly, because people with autism tend to be visual concrete learners (rather than learning through abstract forms like language) we need to teach a new behaviour in visual and concrete ways.

One behaviour which serves a number of different functions cannot necessarily be resolved using the same method if we wish to change it successfully, though in Tommy's case, because both behaviours are related to attention seeking, we can get pretty close. With Tommy, we instituted a behaviour management programme which involved a short period of consistent one-to-one support for him. Although this was both expensive and inconvenient – because it reduced the amount of time we could give to other learners – we accepted that we had to invest the time if we wanted to change the behaviour; and we had to change the behaviour because Tommy was hurting lots of people and getting himself disliked into the bargain! The one-to-one (Janet) started to teach Tommy to stroke her arm as a way of saying hello – by catching his hand as he went to pinch. As she did this she would give him lots of immediate positive attention, through smiling and making a big show of social approval to him. By being with Tommy all of the time, Janet was also able to catch his hand if he caught other adults unawares, stroke it on the adult's arm, who would then also show social approval to Tommy. Gradually, over a period of a couple of weeks, the behaviour started to diminish as Tommy learnt a new way of gaining attention and social approval. Of course there are still times when Tommy pinches, especially when he gets overexcited, but because staff are now aware of this, and because it is now only occasional (he might have a 'pinchy day' once a month), there is no need for the one-to-one and we are almost back to normal.

Attempts at social contact may involve a number of different behaviours, such as repetitive touching, tapping or hitting to get attention, repetitive questioning (guaranteed to get an answer), intense eye contact, without the learner necessarily knowing what to do next. Clearly, many of these behaviours may be considered challenging.

CASE STUDY

Stephen is 14. He has autism and severe learning difficulties, though he is developmentally quite low functioning, operating academically at around P4/P5, with a relatively limited spoken vocabulary.

Stephen loves open spaces and gets very excited when in the playground or the park. He has always loved to be chased and squeals with delight when it is done to him. When he is not being chased, however, he hits other children over the head – very hard – and then runs off. It is also very noticeable that he looks at an adult when he is doing it. Staff have suggested that he's hitting others deliberately because he nearly always laughs as he does it.

Again, it helps if we can work out **Why**. One theory clearly expressed here is that he enjoys the hitting (otherwise, why laugh?) but that doesn't seem to fit in with the fact that he's looking for adult attention as he hits. If he enjoyed the reaction he would look at the child not the adult. A more likely *Why?* is that he wants someone to chase him, and since adults have always chased him when he hits someone – in order to sit him on a 'time-out' bench for 5 minutes – it seems a perfectly reasonable way to continue to communicate that he wants to be chased. At least it's perfectly reasonable from Stephen's perspective, though not from the hit child's perspective. As Stephen is attempting to communicate we need to give him an acceptable method – perhaps by giving a PECS symbol to an adult – and then he needs to be chased! Of course unless the school employs some very fit staff, you might also wish to limit the chasing time, or perhaps encourage his peers to chase him instead, thereby encouraging positive peer interactions as a by-product.

The Picture Exchange Communication System (PECS) (Frost and Bondy 2001) is now a well-established method of communication used by children with autism. Like so many of the autism intervention strategies (TEACCH, ABA, Options) it is an American initiative and is particularly effective at (i) providing a motivational spring to communicating and (ii) giving communicative control to the learner. As the title says, the learner exchanges a picture for an object and although it was initially used with quite high-functioning ASD children, many dual diagnosed (ASD/SLD) pupils will be able to use it to some degree.

In its favour it is very simple, easy to use and understandable to everyone. It is very low tech, relatively cheap, highly adaptable and can be easily used in every situation – school, home, respite, after school clubs, etc. Like signing, it tends to improve verbalisations rather than reduce them and is particularly effective with ASD learners because it does not require direct eye contact and does not rely on understanding social situations or social reward in the same way that speech does. For those with severe learning difficulties it is, however, dependent on the ability to differentiate between symbols, photos and/or objects and is probably not suitable in all its stages for learners operating developmentally at under 3 years. Nonetheless, it can be very useful even at a very basic level of communication. Finally, as with all things relating to teaching autism, it demands **a lot** of organisation and forward planning!

Challenging behaviour and sensory issues

Going back to the case of Tommy, another interesting factor is that he is definitely much more inclined to pinch when he gets overstimulated and as we've noted in Chapter 3 'What is ASD?', controlling changes to the sensory environment and the sensory self do not come easily to those with autism. **It is undoubtedly true that sensory overload is a *major* cause of challenging behaviour in individuals with autism** and teaching children, young people and adults with ASD/SLD **without** taking every opportunity to minimise sensory overload is probably doomed to failure.

For most problems, however, there is a fairly simple solution and the list below, whilst definitely not exhaustive, offers some guidance to dealing with the more common sensory issues. These ideas have been taken from the work of Smith Myles *et al.* (2001) and I would recommend it to you should you need more information than is carried here. It is clear, straightforward and not overly academic and although it is primarily related to Asperger Syndrome, the diagnoses and practical solutions offered apply equally to autism. Particularly interesting is the division into **hyper**-sensitivity – being over-sensitive to particular stimuli – and **hypo**-sensitivity – being under-sensitive to particular stimuli. For ease of understanding, I am just going to refer here to over and under-sensitivity.

Visual (sight) difficulties

People with autism who are visually over-sensitive might well:

- be sensitive to bright (especially fluorescent) lights and flashes;
- have difficulty with both giving and receiving direct eye contact;
- use peripheral vision so that they appear not to be paying attention;
- look at things with a succession of quick glances;
- be fascinated by small things or moving parts;
- examine things in minute detail.

Possible strategies for visual over-sensitivity might include:

- not insisting upon direct eye contact as a sign that the person is concentrating – the instruction to 'Look at me when I'm talking to you' is a familiar one, but may well constitute an impossible task for the autistic individual who might be so busy dealing with the visual overload that they haven't heard a word you say anyway;
- conducting a visual 'risk assessment' so that contact with shiny objects, fluorescent lights, bright colours and reflective surfaces, etc. is avoided as much as possible;
- keeping room displays and decoration to a minimum and not changing the displays/decoration too often;
- using dimmer lights and giving the autistic person the option of wearing sunglasses indoors.

Visually under-sensitive persons might:

- look intensely at lights;
- have difficulty with clear things (water in a glass, glass doors, etc.);
- have difficulty crossing thresholds because, for example, they're unable to perceive changes in lighting (from one room to another) or changes in one form of floor surfacing to another (such as from dark lino to light carpet);
- walk around touching everything in an unfamiliar room;
- move fingers and objects in front of their eyes.

Possible strategies for visual under-sensitivity could be to:

- experiment with lighting so that a balance is found that suits the individual;

- pre-warn in difficult situations, e.g. 'We're going through the door' and *take your time* doing it;

- give a precise running commentary or explanation as a regular additional cue to potentially problematic experiences;

- allow the individual time and opportunity to explore new environments in order to develop a visual map for future reference;

- avoid changes in room lay-out and design.

Auditory (hearing) difficulties

People with autism who are over-sensitive to sound might well:

- put their hands over, or fingers in, their ears;

- have sleep problems;

- dislike certain sounds and/or pitches of sound – especially on the higher registers;

- be fearful of loud noises;

- hum, sing or scream to screen out other noises they're not in control of;

- have difficulty processing some sounds.

There are, however, a number of simple strategies for over-sensitivity to sound (audio hyper-sensitivity) which are fairly easily applied, so that we might:

- whisper or sing instructions;

- encourage the child to wear earplugs or (industrial) headphones as worn by road-diggers;

- pre-warn about loud noises using visual and tactile cues;

- instruct others entering a room not to bang doors or speak too loudly;

- gain the attention of the individual by calling his/her name first, as in 'Toby, please stand up' rather than 'Please stand up, Toby';

- use **exactly** the same language if you're repeating instructions;

- speak clearly using simple unambiguous language;

- support language with signing and symbols;

- avoid crowds, noisy environments, large echoey buildings, etc.

People with autism who are under-sensitive to sound might well:

- ignore loud sounds;

- enjoy loud rhythmic noises;

- be fascinated by trucks, buses, airports and noisy places generally;

- hold sound objects to their ears;

- like machine sounds;

- often create sounds to stimulate hearing.

Possible strategies for under-sensitivity to sound might be:

- to provide opportunities for play with noisy toys or equipment;
- to use loud sounds to encourage social interaction by, for example, taking turns to beat a drum rhythmically;
- to timetable legitimate noisy times.

CASE STUDY

Angus is 6 years old and has been diagnosed with autism and severe learning difficulties. He is at present operating developmentally around P6.

Angus spends most of the day with his fingers in his ears and gets particularly anxious at relatively noisy times of the school day such as lunchtimes, playtimes and assembly. Oddly for someone clearly sensitive to sound, Angus's normal reaction to over-stimulation is to scream very loudly (and then bite the nearest person to hand – or mouth!). His family have stopped taking him out of the house because of his adverse reaction to traffic noises. Generally, however, Angus copes well both at home and in class where both his family and the school staff try to keep the atmosphere ordered, structured, quiet and low key.

Recently, Fahid became a new addition to the class. Fahid also has a dual diagnosis of ASD/SLD and initially settled in very well. Unfortunately he has also recently started to scream, especially when Angus is around. He seems to delight in the chain reaction of him screaming followed by Angus screaming followed by Fahid screaming some more, and has been regularly setting Angus off quite deliberately. The class staff have had a harrowing time of it, trying to keep order in the class and are very conscious that the rest of the children in the class are suffering as a result.

Oh dear! Two screamers in one classroom, both screaming for different reasons, but nonetheless setting each other off, with the additional problem of one of them (Angus) biting both staff and pupils in his distress. Fortunately, this wasn't too difficult to resolve since the reasons why were fairly clear, in that both pupils were the 'cause' of the other's screaming – Fahid screams to 'turn Angus on' (such an exciting switch to have discovered, and it works every time!) – whilst Angus screams to block out the noises he's not in control of. Logically, therefore, we only needed to stop Fahid from screaming and, though 'only' can sometimes be a very big little word and we had to go through several options to get the right one, logic did apply as in most cases involving those on the autistic spectrum.

Initially we started off with a social story (see below) and a behaviour management plan which rewarded Fahid for not screaming for 1 hour – with a 5-minute burst of a Thomas the Tank DVD as his reward – but found that (i) the social story was too complex for Fahid and (ii) the time demanded seemed to be too long – especially first thing in the morning. Operating on the basis that the principles seemed right even though the practice wasn't working, we made the story simpler by using matchstick men drawings rather than words and reduced the time factor to 30 minutes. This proved a bit better, but there were still major problems in the mornings, when Fahid saw Angus for the first time that day. Whilst we could key Fahid in to a certain pattern of behaviour once he was in school, the whole routine of getting up in the morning, going on the bus, coming into school, going to the toilet, coming into class, making Angus scream had become firmly established in Fahid's mind and in order to extinguish the behaviour we would have to break the pattern. Success was finally achieved when we started taking Fahid into a separate room before he went into class with Angus for the first time, where we could then run through the social story and reward him for not screaming. Just to be on the safe side, we also initially brought Fahid into class for shortened staggered periods, so that each morning he came in for 5 minutes with 5 minutes out on reward, then 10 minutes with 5 minutes out on reward, then 20 minutes with 5 minutes out on reward, before settling into the class for the day at 10.00 a.m. This also proved successful so that we were gradually able to reduce Fahid's time out of class.

As is so often the case with challenging behaviour – and especially so given the very powerful reward Angus gives to Fahid whenever he screams – three steps forward is accompanied by one step back, and there were some occasions when Fahid found it impossible to resist screaming. But overall the screaming reduced significantly in quite a short space of time – a couple of weeks – and because there was a programme in place, class staff always had something to fall back on if the behaviour reappeared more than just occasionally.

Tactile difficulties

People with autism who are over-sensitive to touch might:

- not like being hugged or touched, or not like certain parts of their body touched and generally have problems with skin against skin;
- dislike washing hair or cutting nails;
- refuse to wear certain clothes and/or become obsessive about wearing particular items of clothing (to death!);
- strip off their clothing and/or constantly take off their shoes irrespective of the weather or conditions underfoot;
- overreact to small injuries and to variations in temperature;
- be obsessive about washing and keeping clean;
- avoid getting messy, being put into situations where they might get messy or having to touch materials like paint and glue, etc.

Possible strategies for those over-sensitive to touch will include:

- keeping touch brief and firm;
- giving individuals 'space' – don't crowd in or get too close when working;
- being aware that there will be times and places (like assemblies, for example) which are going to be difficult for those sensitive to touch;
- ensuring that shoes and socks are comfortable;

- choosing clothes carefully and perhaps opting for soft fabrics – though this will be a matter of trial and error;
- keeping the room temperature constant (and perhaps on the low side);
- introducing messy activities *very* gradually;
- trying to cut nails when the child is sleeping;
- establishing what method of touch and degree of pressure is tolerable for each individual.

Those under-sensitive to touch might:

- appear not to feel pain;
- self-injure;
- ignore injuries;
- be indifferent to temperature change;
- be hyperactive;
- like pressure especially in the form of wearing tight clothes or rough and tumble.

Possible strategies for the tactilely under-sensitive should include:

- providing alternatives to self-injurious behaviour, for example things to bite on or things to hit/punch (and, of course, time to do this);
- being vigilant about injuries;
- timetabling regular activity sessions or firm massage;
- teaching about hot and cold;
- teaching about the appropriateness of physical contact and personal space.

Temple Grandin, an American autistic woman and the author of several books on the subject (for example, Grandin and Scariano (1986) and Grandin (2006)), has famously built a 'squeeze machine' in her house. The idea for the machine was taken from those used on American cattle ranches where the cow is led into an enclosed space prior to branding. A lever is pulled and the sides of the fencing squeeze the cow keeping her enclosed and still. Temple noted how much this contraption calmed the cattle, who were obviously in a state of some arousal prior to the branding, and therefore designed a similar machine for herself which she uses successfully when she feels in need of calming. Other strategies can be used which don't involve building a 'squeeze machine' and particularly successful are weighted coats; hats that are a size too small; lycra; squeezing a large physiotherapy ball over a prone pupil; squeezing pupils between PE mats. Clearly the common factor in all of these techniques is that they give pressure (like a hug) but do not involve direct human contact.

Gustatory (taste)

Those with sensitivities in this area might:

- have food fads – it **has** to be McCain's oven chips, it **must** be Heinz baked beans;
- have difficulties in properly digesting gluten found in cereals, or casein found in cow's milk;
- eat indiscriminately;
- hold food in their mouths for long periods of time;
- gag, vomit and/or regurgitate food.

Christopher Boone, the hero of *The Curious Incident of the Dog in the Night-Time*, will not eat anything yellow. In fact yellow is his most hated colour so that the 'badness' of the day ahead is dictated by how many yellow cars he sees on his way to school. Four yellow cars is a **very bad day** indeed!

Possible strategies to help those who are taste sensitive should include:

- seeking the advice of a Speech and Language Therapist (SALT) trained in devising eating and drinking programmes (not all SALTs are);
- seeking the advice of a dietician;
- introducing new foods **very** slowly and **very** gradually;
- rewarding pupils for eating **very** small quantities of unfamiliar foodstuffs with what they like to eat;
- having regular routines at mealtimes so that as many things are as constant and predictable as possible when new foods are introduced;
- being conscious of the autistic person's preferences and not ignoring them!

It is still a source of some amazement to me that a child can survive on a diet exclusively made up of toast and Marmite, Pringle's crisps and strawberry milkshakes!

Olfactory (smell)

Those with sensitivities in this area might:

- sniff, smell and/or lick people and things. This can be **very** embarrassing, especially if the thing being smelt is your armpit or (even worse) your bottom! The more so if the smelling takes place in the middle of Sainsbury's!;
- insist on wearing the same (unwashed) clothes day after day after day after . . .;
- alternatively, dislike strong smells.

Possible strategies to help those who are smell sensitive:

- social stories might be effective here if you really **have** to change the behaviour, though as with all behaviours – don't change it if you don't have to!

Physical

Difficulties here will usually be related to the kinaesthetic areas of the vestibular sense (balance and where we are in relation to other things around us) and the proprioceptive sense (how our bodies connect together to form the whole – where my elbow is in relation to my shoulder, etc.). Many of those on the autistic continuum have difficulties with:

- especially gross (but also fine) motor coordination;
- appearing clumsy and awkward, typically knocking things over or bumping into things and/or people;
- appearing to have 'strange' movement patterns;
- indulging in stereotypical and repetitive movements such as rocking.

There has been some interesting work done on sensory integration by occupational therapists inspired by Jean Ayres, for example Ayres *et al.* (2004). Ayres argues that sensory experiences include touch, movement, body position, vision, smell, taste, sound and the pull of gravity. The process of the brain organising and interpreting this information is called sensory integration, which provides a crucial foundation for later, more complex learning and behaviour. For most children sensory integration develops in the course of ordinary childhood activities, but for some children sensory integration does not develop as efficiently as it should. This is known as dysfunction in sensory integration (DSI). When the process is disordered a number of problems in learning, motor skills and behaviour may be evident.

Some signs of dysfunction in sensory integration might be:

- physical clumsiness;
- difficulty learning new movements;
- unusually high or low activity level;
- poor body awareness;
- inappropriate response to touch, movements, sights or sounds;
- poor self-esteem;
- social and/or emotional difficulties.

Ayres argues that the experiences naturally gone through in childhood, especially those related to physical movements such as being held and cuddled, being carried, being swung as a baby both sideways and back and forth, sitting atop an adult's shoulders, etc., are often denied to many (an autistic child) because of their aversion to close physical contact. These experiences are, however, necessary for both physical and emotional development and need to be experienced if the child is to grow. The answer, she states, is in her sensory integration programme and the concentration on both the vestibular and proprioceptive systems.

As I said, the theory is interesting, and on the face of it, seems to carry some considerable logic. There has, however, still not been enough independent research to be sure of its effectiveness, though this certainly shouldn't stop you using it.

Challenging behaviour and problems with transition and unplanned change

> ### CASE STUDY
>
> Mario is 8 years old. He has a diagnosis of ASD with additional learning difficulties, is functioning around P7/P8, and is currently in a mainstream primary class with 25 other pupils. The LEA have allocated 15 hours of TA time to work specifically with Mario, but there is another full-time TA supporting another child in the class with Down Syndrome and she may be able to share some of the load.
>
> Mario certainly needs all the support he can get, because he is a constant disruption during lessons and is always 'agenda setting' – that is, he is very happy working at what **he** wants to do (which is more or less anything to do with dinosaurs) but is extremely reluctant to get involved with any 'normal' work. Even when he does he is constantly getting up from his desk and moving around the room unable seemingly to concentrate on task. This is especially so during whole-class tasks when Mario doesn't appear to listen to instructions and is unable to get on with work. He also has a great deal of difficulty in completing work set and can often get quite violent when asked to finish it.

Mainstream setting or not, the principles still apply and in this case it is pretty clear that Mario is 'lost'. Not literally of course, though he might as well be, because for someone with autism a large classroom can be a very strange place, especially when you don't know what to do. A large classroom (any classroom in fact) is full of potential sensory, communicative and social confusions – there are places to sit (where?); people to sit next to (who?); things to prepare (what?), (are they the same as yesterday or the day before?); voices to listen to (who is more important?); information to act upon (which applies to me?); tasks to undertake (who, what, where, why and when??). I'm confused and I'm merely writing it!

People with autism don't necessarily have the ability to deal with the flexibility of thought and action required within a normal classroom setting. If things change daily and indeed hourly, they have no reference point to come back to. Just the fact that children might well sit in different places during circle time – because they're now best friends with somebody else; because it's a slightly different group setting; because somebody is off sick – is quite enough to throw a number of autistics into a welter of confusion.

Their communicative and sensory disabilities are likely to make it extremely difficult for them to attend/concentrate in any size of group of more than three or four for any length of time. They will probably need lots of time-outs to gather thoughts and ease the stress. They will need certainty in every area of their day – even down to where they have to sit (perhaps by sticking a cross on the floor with tape, X marks the spot).

Enter the timetable – and because children, young people and adults with autism learn best in a concrete visual way – enter the visual timetable.

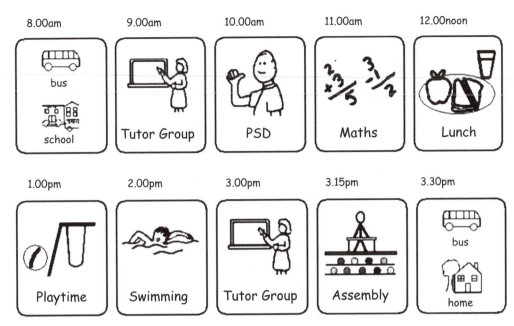

Figure 7.1   Visual timetable for the day

The visual timetable will probably need to be gone through **at least** once a day and probably far more often than that, though this will obviously depend on the degree of learning difficulty and the ability of the individual to retain the information. Even when the timetable has been learnt, going through it regularly will provide considerable reassurance that things have not changed. For those with additional learning difficulties and those with particularly high anxiety about potential changes, it may also be necessary to provide a timetable within a timetable (Figure 7.2).

10.00am 1st session till 11.00am

Figure 7.2   Visual timetable for the hour

Visual timetables are very effective within classrooms housing autistic people because they:

● provide structure;

- avoid confrontation;
- remove constant questioning;
- prepare for change;
- encourage appropriate and expected behaviour.

It is undoubtedly true that SLD classes have also benefited greatly from their introduction even when there are no autistic children in the group, because those with SLD also learn best when taught in a concrete visual way.

But of course Mario's difficulties are about more than just the need for certainty and order in the daily routine; they are also about the certainty of words. What exactly does 'work' mean? What exactly does 'finished' mean? Work to a gardener could be relaxation to a teaching assistant – or it could be 'What's going on? Not the grass needing cutting again!' And when exactly have you finished cutting the grass? When it's looking shorter than before? When there are beautiful lines going up and down? When the edges have been trimmed to precisely 3 centimetres long? Words like 'work' and 'finished' are of course subjective, contextual and, to a large degree, abstract. That means that they may, or may not, have meaning to someone with autism, but that meaning is likely to be different to your meaning – especially when he/she desperately wants to get on the computer to look at the dinosaur website. We therefore have to be **very** careful when using language and be clear that we have a **shared meaning** with the autistic person. Probably the best way we can do this is to give the word precision as in 'Mario must work for 20 minutes' (assuming that is a realistically achievable target) and 'When Mario works for 20 minutes, his work is finished'. We can then add 'When Mario works for 20 minutes, Mario can have 5 minutes on the dinosaur website'. We might also need to support the meaning of the phrases '20 minutes' and '5 minutes' with additional concrete clues, such as appropriate visual timers.

Challenging behaviour and panic, fears and phobias

We have already established that people with autism can often be in a state of high anxiety which might well lead to panic and (naturally) displays of challenging behaviour, though this might be complicated by the panic being brought about by a phobic experience. Whitaker (2001) notes the high preponderance of phobias among people with autism and remarks that the autistic person may well develop associations with the situation or place where the fear has occurred, which may well complicate the issue. Identifying the source of the fear is therefore important, if it can be done. He goes on to suggest a programme of gradual desensitisation and Jordan (2001) advises on coupling this with the teaching of coping strategies. If the person has a fear of dogs, for example, Jordan suggests that you might seat them in a quiet darkened room, softly playing some favoured music and then flash up a very small picture of a dog for 1 second. The next day you might do the same for 2 seconds, and so on. Gradually you would increase the size of the picture, and then maybe introduce a video. The whole experience needs to be as reassuring and non-confrontational as possible, and to be done **very** slowly. You might never overcome the fear totally, but at least you may be able to teach some coping strategies and give the person very many opportunities of practising such coping strategies in secure situations.

Consistency

For the autistic learner, consistency is about much more than everyone following the same policy – though that is, of course, still essential – it is also about keeping our dealings with them consistent and their lives as ordered, structured and, most importantly, as predictable as possible. Like those with a profound learning difficulty, when you're not in control of what's happening within your own life, you need to be sure that those who are in control (us) are doing a really good job. Life for the autistic person is hard enough, without springing surprises on them.

Positive

For those with autism, punishing challenging behaviour – in, for example, the form of ignoring, telling off, withdrawing privileges, etc. – is a particularly pointless act because it doesn't teach the person what they should be doing, it merely tells them what they should not be doing. Children, young people and adults with autism **by definition** lack the social imagination, communicative and interactive skills to change it **by themselves.** They, therefore, need us to show them what to do and we can only do that if we teach a more positive approach. Further, because autistic people are very much creatures of habit, and bad habits are as easily established as good habits, not replacing a bad habit just doesn't make sense. If we use punishment as a core factor, the behaviour will always resurface, because we are waiting for it to happen before we act. Sometimes the punishment can be incredibly rewarding – as we've already seen with Tommy's pinching and Fahid's screaming. If we are to extinguish (get rid of) the behaviour in the long term, we must be prepared to teach an alternative behaviour which has the same rewards for the individual.

Reward

Wendy Lawson, who has Asperger's herself, talks of the over-arching importance of the autistic person's special interests and describes autistic people as being mono-tropic (Lawson 2001). This opposes to non-autistic people who are poly-tropic, that is who have many areas of interest which, in turn, leads to other interests. Somebody (like me, for example) might be interested (in no particular order) in reading, work, current affairs, gardening, sport, cars, family and music. These interests represent the main branches of a tree. One branch, the musical interest, for example, might have all sorts of smaller branches growing out of it like jazz, pop, soul, classical, folk, etc. One smaller branch, like jazz, may have all sorts of twigs growing out of it that are perhaps represented by particular artists like Keith Jarrett, Miles Davis, Esborn Svensson, Kurt Elling, etc. These poly-tropic interests represent a large and many-branched tree, with many sub-branches, twigs and leaves to make the whole.

The mono-tropic interest(s) of the autistic person however make for a single trunk, or perhaps one that divides into two – no sub-branches, no twigs, no leaves. The 'musical' interests of the autistic person start and stop at Michael Jackson and there are no sub-divisions or spin-offs from this. It would indeed probably be mistaken to assume that this is a musical interest at all; it is an interest – a very, very special interest in the same way as Thomas the Tank is a very, very special interest, or trampolining is a very, very special interest or sliding metal bolts back and forth is a very, very special interest.

In some ways this presents problems because like Mario with his dinosaurs all he wants to work on is his very, very special interest, but (and this is a very, very special but) the power of the interest is a fantastic way of changing behaviour because it becomes an incredibly effective reward. If there is a drawback to the guaranteed existence of such a powerful motivator it is that you might well have problems in finishing the reward, but as long as the same principles of shared meaning are established (by, for example, time-limiting the reward) there shouldn't be too many problems.

Control

In many ways much of the challenging behaviour exhibited by those on the autistic spectrum is about control as much as it is about anything. The high state of anxiety experienced by many is naturally going to lead to behaviours which try and reduce the anxiety – especially if we (as their teaching partners) are not able or willing to provide a calm, ordered, secure and comfortable environment. Much as someone might bite their nails, pace the room, light up a cigarette, pick their skin or seek a reassuring cuddle from a partner or parent in moments of high tension, so the autistic person might well revert to tried and trusted repetitive/obsessive behaviours which can 'block out' or at least reduce the uncertainty and anxiety. This might also be their mono-tropic interest which can also serve as a tension reducer – again much the same as a crossword puzzle, a sudoku or just a calming cup of tea and chat with a friend. The autistic person's need to maintain control is no different from the non-autistic person's need to maintain control. The only difference is that the autistic person is seldom in control, and the 'controlling' behaviours can often stop anything else from happening – which might, after all, be their purpose.

As with severe learning difficulties, it should not be our intention to take the control away – surely we all have a right to take some control over our lives – but we might need to bring in a shared meaning, by, for example, allocating a set amount of time for the 'controlling' behaviour. Mario can choose to have 5 minutes on his dinosaur website when he's done 20 minutes of work, both timed with a sand-timer and noted on his visual timetable. Equally, we should look to providing safe areas for those who need to have time away from the hustle and bustle and sensory confusion of the classroom. It doesn't have to be a specific time-out room, though if you have the space it could be, but access to it does need to be in the control of the autistic person. Again a shared meaning of how long and when it should be used needs to be put in place.

Time

Because people with autism generally respond so positively to a reward led system of changing behaviour, you should see a significant change within a fairly short space of time (certainly within 4 weeks) and sometimes almost instantaneously, **provided**:

1   the learner understands what's expected of him;

2   you've got the reason for the behaviour right;

3   you're able to control the reasons (which may not always be possible with sensory issues);

4   you've got the rewards right.

As with both SLD and PMLD, the long-term strategy must always be for the learner to take control of their own behaviour, but people with autism can only do that if we are able and willing to provide the conditions under which they can learn effectively.

Success

It can often appear that life is so easy for a writer who presents case studies of challenging behaviour. The problem arises, everyone gathers around being positive, suggestions are made which work instantly, the child is 'cured' and everyone lives happily ever after. If only! Life is just not like that. There is undoubtedly, however, a curve of experience, where the more you apply the principles the fewer the failures and the more long lived the successes. Regressions do occur, but this is no different from regressions in other areas of learning. A child who slips behind in his/her reading having been previously successful can catch up, given an amount of remedial support and attention to the detail of what worked before. Babies who are learning to walk don't suddenly become adept at the practice over night. It takes time and patience and persistence and many, many falls.

Finally in this chapter, it might be worth a quick perusal of strategies already existing that are tried and tested. In other words – what works?

Know about autism!

It would be extremely difficult (and in many, many ways highly undesirable) to take on a job teaching German without knowing a word of the language. I'm not suggesting that it would take as long to learn about autism as it might do to learn German, though some will say it will certainly take longer! The principle applies, however, that the more you know about autism, and the more you put the basic rules of structure, order, certainty and low arousal into place, the easier it will be. By reading the chapters on autism in this book, you will probably have the equivalent of a basic smattering of holiday German – enough to get you to the train station and buy yourself a cup of coffee in a restaurant – but that's about all. If you're serious about working with children, young people or adults with autism – read more, go on courses, attend conferences!

Keep your class size small

On the basis that most people reading this book will probably be working in special schools, it seems to make sense to advise on a general rule of keeping the autistic class size to a maximum of six pupils. This is of course an arbitrary number in many ways, but many years of practical experience at The Bridge School working with autistic children – most of whom have moderate or severe learning difficulties – leads to this conclusion. Numbers higher than that have generally led to problems in the past, unless it is an exceptionally able and untroubled class. If you have it as a rule, you can always break the rule, though be very, very careful of doing so.

No doubt the reader working in mainstream will be sighing 'Six! What bliss!' but remember that this is six all with autism and additional learning difficulties. It is not my intention here to enter into the inclusion debate and I am certainly not suggesting that children with autism cannot be successfully educated in the mainstream class. However, because children with autism tend to find it difficult to function effectively in large groups, individual learning time within a smaller group (say three or four at most) will need to be built in and your child may need to have access to a time-out room; whether the education is taking place in a mainstream or a special school setting.

Reduce sensory confusion

Whatever the class size, you have to ensure order, structure, consistency and low arousal for the autistic child or children. The same applies at home or in the respite centre.

TEACCH

TEACCH stands for the Treatment and Education of Autistic and related Communication-handicapped CHildren. There are a number of defining principles:

- Diagnosis and individual assessment are essential.
- There is a strong focus on emerging skills.
- The stress is on the autistic person's understanding of what is expected rather than purely on the principle of positive reward, though reward for completing work does feature.
- There is a strong respect for the learning styles and needs of the autistic individual.
- There is an emphasis on classroom arrangement and daily schedules so that there are constant clues as to what is expected. This gives freedom from the autistic anxiety of what is going to happen next.

- There is a strong work ethic and a philosophy of 'work now, play later'.
- Spoken language is reduced as much as possible.

Most people will be familiar with the TEACCH classroom and its individual learning stations, low-stimulation environment, regular referral to visual timetables and different coloured trays for work to be done and work completed. When the work is done it is placed in the *work done* tray and the next piece of work is taken out of the *work to be done* tray. When a set amount of work is done the child is rewarded.

There seems little doubt that children with autism respond extremely positively to the TEACCH methodology and it seems to have a proven record on reducing anxiety and therefore challenging behaviours, though there has to date been no major independent study verifying its effectiveness (Jones 2002). There are some criticisms, the major one being that such strict order, structure and certainty is not the real world, though this doesn't alter the fact that the best bits do work. I am not here necessarily recommending TEACCH as a requirement for the autistic person, more suggesting that what works for TEACCH – order, structure and certainty being the main elements – should form the basic criteria of every autistic environment. As Whitaker (2001) has pointed out 'children with autistic spectrum disorders need structure' (p. 35), but how that structure is given could be through other means. The Autistic Society, for example, (www.nas.org.uk) suggests a system called SPELL which advises having Structure, being Positive, being Empathetic to the individual autistic person, ensuring Low arousal and pursuing Links with our non-autistic society.

Social stories

Carol Gray's social stories (Gray 2000) are not so much stories in the accepted sense as guidelines shared with an autistic individual as to what is expected of him/her in a given situation. In other words, they're stories telling him/her what to do and how to behave. This may sound particularly prescriptive, but that is exactly their strength, because a person who has little or no understanding of social situations needs all the help he/she can get.

The story is written (or possibly drawn for younger and/or less able individuals) according to specific guidelines which describe a situation in terms of relevant cues and common responses. The underlying philosophy stresses the importance of *abandoning all assumptions,* that is assuming that the autistic person has absolutely no understanding of what to do or what other people expect of him/her. It seeks to (i) understand the student's perspective (ii) ensure a student has the social information that he/she needs and (iii) present information that is accessible and easily understood. As a result social stories have a reassuring, accepting quality through positively and matter-of-factly describing a specific event.

Whilst social stories are normally written for individual students (though they could be written for a group) and are designed to reflect an understanding of the student's unique perception of a situation, this may not be easy to ascertain. Considering the social communication impairment in autism, determining a student's perspective can be difficult and it is sometimes helpful to illustrate a conversation like a comic strip.

There are essentially four types of sentence used and descriptive and/or perspective sentences should outnumber directive or control sentences. The types of sentence are:

1   descriptive – describing the events;
2   perspective – of the autistic person as well as others involved in the social situation;
3   directive – what the autistic person needs to do;
4   control – strategies which might help the autistic person remember what to do.

Carol Gray gives an example of Mary's problems in coming into the class from the playground and sets out the story as follows:

Descriptive sentences

The bell rings for the children to come in from break. The children go to their classroom where the teacher reads a story.

Perspective sentences

When the bell rings for break to end, the teacher is happy to see all the children line up quietly and walk to their classroom. Many children are excited that they get to hear a story. The teacher likes to see the children listen. The teacher likes it when children are quiet during the story.

Directive sentences

When the bell rings, I stop playing and line up to come in. I follow the other children and quietly go to the classroom. When we get to the classroom, I go to my desk and sit down. I listen as my teacher reads a story.

Control sentences

I remember that the bell means it's time for break to end by thinking of a teapot. I know that when it whistles, the water is done. The bell is like the whistle; when it rings, break is done.

Implementing a social story

For an autistic person who can read, the author might introduce the story by reading it twice through. The autistic person then might read it once a day independently. For someone who cannot read, the author might read the story on an audiotape with cues for the person to turn the page as he/she 'reads' along. These cues could be a bell or a verbal statement when it is time to turn the page. The person listens and 'reads' along with the story once a day.

Establishing the story

Once the autistic individual successfully enacts the skills or appropriately responds to the social situation, the story can be faded out. This can be done by reducing the number of times the story is read during the week and only reviewing the story once a month or as necessary. Fading can also be accomplished by rewriting the story, gradually removing directive sentences from the story.

Summary

This chapter has tried to give some ideas around dealing effectively with challenging behaviours exhibited by those with a diagnosis of autism. They may also have an additional severe or profound learning difficulty and indeed all strategies are suggested with this context in mind. But with autism, it is the autism that has to be addressed first and the learning difficulty second. The existence of the autism will always take precedence over the learning difficulty and you cannot expect that strategies effective with SLD or PMLD pupils will be equally effective with ASD pupils. They may be, but you cannot expect it.

It is **absolutely** essential that you make every effort to establish why the behaviour is occurring in the first place. It is likely that the very considerable difficulties faced by the autistic child, young person or adult in communication, social interaction, flexibility of thought and action and sensory overload will hold the key to the **Why?** As with both SLD and PMLD there will **always** be a reason and it is very likely that when looked at from the child's perspective, that reason will be perfectly rational. That is, it will be consistent with the autism.

As with both SLD and PMLD, the key to success lies in **teaching new behaviours** in ways that are empathetic to the autism. Individuals with autism and SLD cannot just inhibit behaviours; they will tend to continue with the behaviour no matter how much it is punished. The behaviour may become habitual and they lack the social imagination, communicative and interactive skills to change it. The behaviour will therefore tend to remain because they don't know what else to do.

Writing a behaviour management programme

Although this is not a particularly difficult practice, it is one that is absolutely essential to the success of any strategies devised. If you take as a general rule that if *it's not written down, it's not going to happen,* writing it down effectively becomes doubly important. This chapter is, however, one of the shortest in the whole book for the very simple reason that to be effective, the behaviour management programme needs to be a **very** short document. It should contain:

1 a couple of sentences of background information, including some ideas as to why (you think) the behaviour is occurring;

2 a single objective, though definitely only two at the most;

3 some suggestions about how you're going to help the child, young person or adult to achieve the target;

4 the initials of the person writing the programme;

5 the date.

Let's take these issues one by one.

1 A couple of sentences of background information, including some ideas as to why (you think) the behaviour is occurring

Not everyone who deals with the child, young person or adult who displays challenging behaviours is going to know them equally well. A little bit of information for those who might not be in the normal information loop, such as meal supervisors or bus escorts at school or occasional supply cover at the respite home, is always helpful. Clearly you're going to have to be selective about what you say and confidential information cannot be given out in such a document, but *why?* has to be addressed. You may want to try and be specific, especially if the child has ASD, as in 'Liam really enjoys watching Jonathon going into a tantrum' as a reason behind Liam hitting Jonathon over the head with the nearest available object, or fall back on attention seeking and/or task avoidance if you're referring to someone with SLD or PMLD. Either way, it is always best to try for a reason, otherwise the reader might assume that there is no reason at all, and we know (don't we!) that this is definitely **not** the case.

2 A single objective, though definitely only two at the most

A key factor in any behaviour management programme is to make absolutely sure that it's a success. We can get overwhelmed with the multiplicity of behaviours and problems and if we try to solve everything at once we're likely to end up solving nothing. Write a hierarchy of behaviours, detailing the 'worst' behaviour, the one most in need of changing, and concentrate on that single behaviour. Be successful with that one and move on to the next. Of course it may be that all the behaviours can be resolved by a single action plan (as for example with Rahul in Chapter 4 and Tina (though much slower) in Chapter 5), though most often this is not, unfortunately, the case!

The objective needs to be SMART – Specific, Measurable, Achievable, Realistic and Time-bound. Being wishy-washy with the target is not going to help anyone because this usually means it is impossible to achieve. If Liam is hitting Jonathon several times a day (in order to watch him going into a tantrum) this is clearly an established behaviour and it is probably not realistic to think/hope that this will cease immediately. It may, however, be realistic to expect Liam not to hit Jonathon for an hour – by, for example, establishing a clear system of rewarding Liam for not hitting, perhaps backed up by a social story. *To not hit Jonathon* is **not** specific, **not** achievable, **not** realistic and **not** time-bound. It is measurable, but the measurement is almost inevitably going to indicate failure. By limiting the demands placed on Liam, as in *To not hit Jonathon for 1 hour*, we're trying to ensure that the programme is successful, where success is measured by a reduction in the number of hitting incidents. The greater the success, the more we can move Liam along, so that the next BMP might have as its objective *To not hit Jonathon for 2 hours*.

3 Some suggestions about how you're going to help the child, young person or adult to achieve the target

Firstly you'll need to know the nature of the learning difficulty, in order to opt for the appropriate response, since we have already established that any resolution to the problems of the challenging behaviour will vary according to the nature of that learning difficulty. Secondly, it would certainly be useful to check off 'The Magnificent Seven' – **Why?**, **Consistency**, **Positive**, **Reward**, **Control**, **Time** and **Success**.

Why?

You will need to have some ideas as to why the behaviour is occurring – you may not be correct, but an educated guess is better than no guess at all, because **there is** a reason for the behaviour.

Consistency

You will need to make sure that everyone within the organisation who has regular contact with the child, young person or adult who displays the challenging behaviour(s) is willing and able to follow the same programme. The more people who follow it, the quicker the new behaviour will become established.

Positive

Part of this consistency of approach is to ensure that everyone is adopting a positive attitude to the child and the programme you have adopted. The very best way to do this is to involve as many people as possible in the actual devising of the programme. If people have had a chance to discuss the issues they will feel much more involved and have a common ownership of the programme. It will be **their** programme that has to work rather than a programme imposed on them from above.

Reward

Most programmes, especially for those with SLD and ASD, will involve a reward system. As we have already noted a reward is only a reward if it changes the behaviour, and it therefore has to be motivating to the person whose behaviour you want to change. The very best way of working out what motivates is to devise a **strengths chart** which will detail what the individual is good at. These strengths:

- must be positive;
- can be what the learner enjoys doing as well as what he/she is good at. This may include stereotypical or self-stimulatory behaviours such as 'loves playing with cassette recorders' or 'really enjoys flapping with a favourite piece of string';
- may be associated with spending time with a favourite person or persons, especially if it is an attention-seeking behaviour you're trying to change;
- need not be academic skills – 'has a sense of humour' is a strength;
- should number around ten – you might have to think a bit! – though they may number less for those on the autistic continuum where it might only be one or two;
- will then form the basis for our reward system. You may not be able to use all of them but there will usually be at least a couple that can be used in all situations.

If you **really** can't find any rewards that work it may be that the learner has a profound learning difficulty and therefore can't make the cause and effect connection between the reward and the behaviour. Alternatively – and especially if the learner is diagnosed ASD, or exhibits strong autistic type behaviours, or what works as a reward one day doesn't work the next – it may be that the learner has a tendency towards Pathological Demand Avoidance (PDA). Have a look at Elizabeth Newson's website at pdacontact.org.uk.

Control

If you have established (or even if you believe) that one of the reasons behind the behaviour is that the learner is trying to establish control – however badly – you will need to allow for that control to be exercised effectively in a non-challenging manner. **Please remember** that we shouldn't be aiming to take the control away from the learner, merely to allow him/her to exercise the control without hitting, biting, scratching, kicking, throwing computers over or whatever the behaviours happen to be.

Time

There is virtually always some sort of time factor involved in a behavioural objective. This usually involves the objective itself as in for Liam *To not hit Jonathon for 1 hour*, though you may also wish to outline how you're going to explain time to the learner. To this end sand-timers; clocks which colour in the time as the hand goes round; traffic-light timers which give an amber warning for when the time is nearly up (especially useful for counting down on a reward that the learner might not want to leave); and visual timetables are especially important. **Please remember** that time is a very abstract concept and needs to be explained in a very concrete manner to learners with severe learning difficulties. The second part of the *Time* factor is that for those with a severe learning difficulty, the behaviour should start to change fairly quickly – within 4 weeks at most. If there's been no significant change within that time, it's probable that something basic has gone wrong – the rewards aren't working (they're the wrong 'rewards'), people are being inconsistent in the application of the programme or the objective is too difficult for the learner are the usual ones, but there may be other reasons. Don't give up – try a new tack.

Success

There is no point in putting in place any programme which **cannot** succeed. You may not be absolutely certain that it will succeed, we seldom are, but you should have a good idea that it should succeed. If it doesn't, don't give up: start again – this can be a valuable learning process for all of us. **Please remember**, however, that this is not just about the learner being successful. We cannot and **must not** put all of the emphasis for success on the learner and then blame the learner when it goes wrong. If a behaviour management programme goes wrong, it is virtually always **our** fault, in that we haven't yet found the key. I firmly believe that there is no such thing as a child, young person or adult with a severe or profound learning difficulty who **wants** to display challenging behaviours. They do what they do because they haven't found a better way. It is our job to teach them that better way.

4 The initials of the person writing the programme

Although the devising of the programme should be a collective process involving as many people as possible and certainly all those who regularly come into contact with the learner, the actual writing of the programme needs to be a managerial responsibility. Somebody needs to draw the ideas together and put them down on paper.

5 The date

A simple and obvious detail I know, but I've lost count of how many programmes I've seen that are undated. How do you know which is current? Behaviour management is difficult enough without us adding to the problems!

Finally in this very short chapter, a quote from Dave Hewett (1988a):

> *Many staff, understandably, want to be told exactly what to do when 'this' or 'that' happens. This can be achieved up to a point, and the more effective teams talk about and/or write sensible guiding procedures for known recurring situations. However, expecting to be absolutely and precisely guided in all of the behaviours that you as a member of staff will need in a situation is generally a mistake. It is more realistic and effective for staff to carry with them in their heads a set of principles for managing difficult situations. The principles offer a framework of decision making throughout the incident, but it is necessary to make judgements and decisions based on these principles and the existence of any helpful known procedures.*

(p. 71)

In other words, when dealing with behaviours which challenge us, we need to stay calm and we need to use our common sense. If Liam has gone 55 minutes without hitting Jonathon and you can see him *winding up* for an attack it's probably best to slip into Plan B. You might try distracting or guiding him away from Jonathon, taking Jonathon out of the room for a while or maybe even pretending that the hour is actually up after 55 minutes and giving Liam lots of praise and his reward. Consistency is important but rigidity is not.

Summary

In this chapter, I have tried to give some guidance for actually writing the behaviour management programme itself; and it is **absolutely essential** that it is written down.

The general rules are:

- Try and work out why the behaviour is occurring.
- Do not try and resolve everything at once.
- Organise a priority of behaviours.
- Deal with the single most challenging behaviour first, then move on to the next when success has been achieved.
- Ensure that the objective is SMART.
- Write down some ways in which you might help the learner to achieve the objective.
- Children, young people and adults with severe and profound learning difficulties cannot do it on their own – they have severe and profound learning difficulties!
- If the strategies fail it is almost always our fault.
- Don't give up – try again.

- It doesn't help to be totally rigid in our thinking. We need to be consistent, but we also need to allow for some flexibility. The important feature here is that the learner needs to succeed, and we have to make it as easy as possible for that to happen. Then we can move on to the next (more challenging) target.

- Behaviour management programmes should essentially be about short-term needs and you will therefore have to see some success within a fairly short space of time – probably within a maximum of 4 weeks.

- It is important to have a long-term view and for those with profound learning difficulties there may **only** be a long-term view. For those with severe learning difficulties, however, (with or without autism) you are unlikely to be able to resolve the long-term problems until you resolve the short-term problems.

What do we do when it doesn't work?

Unfortunately, there is no such thing as a fool-proof strategy, and there is no such thing as a book which has all the answers – including (however reluctant I am to write such a statement) this one! I am, however, confident enough to suggest that if the strategies put in place have not worked it is usually something fairly simple and a quick referral back to 'The Magnificent Seven' of **Why?**, **Consistency**, **Positive**, **Reward**, **Control**, **Time** and **Success** may be enough to rectify the problem and should certainly be your first port of call. As mentioned in the last chapter the problems are often fairly simply resolved.

The rewards aren't working

This means effectively that they're the wrong 'rewards' because they are not sufficiently motivating to the individual concerned. Generally with those on the autistic continuum, you're unlikely to have that problem because once you've found the one or possibly two things they **really** like, they'll continue to be highly motivated by them. There is always the chance that the motivator (the individual's very special interest) will change suddenly, but then it's just a matter of switching to the new one. With SLD it may be that they've become bored with the reward, especially if they're receiving it several times a day! There are only so many times you can listen to 'Is this the way to Amarillo?' even if you're a 12-year-old with severe learning difficulties. In this case, try broadening the choices on offer, or have several cards with three or four options on each. The more you know about the child and the sort of things they like, the easier it will be.

The objective is too loose

If the objective is open to interpretation and not **really** tight, it may be that the learner has lost concentration before he/she can achieve it, or doesn't actually understand what the objective is. Generally the answer is to make it time bound as in *to stay on task for 20 minutes.*

The objective is too difficult for the learner

There is often a temptation to say that because a learner can achieve a certain target **most** of the time, he/she should be able to achieve it **all** of the time. That is, our natural desire as educators to stretch our charges can lead to us pushing too hard too fast. Remember that the behaviour is likely to be a very important part of the learner's armoury for survival and he/she will not give it up lightly. We have to make it as easy as possible for him/her to succeed. Once that limited initial success has been achieved **then** we can push a bit harder, but we must **establish** the new behaviour first, which could take several weeks or even months. There should be some changes fairly quickly but **establishing** those changes might take considerably longer.

There may of course be other reasons; and it's always a good idea to talk to as many people as possible to canvass alternative views and try out different strategies. We would after all do exactly that if a learner was unable to learn a particular aspect of the curriculum. Surely we wouldn't continue with teaching strategies and practices that patently didn't work. We'd go back to the beginning, work out where we went wrong, talk to others who are experienced in the field, try different approaches. Teaching appropriate behaviour to people with severe or profound learning difficulties is no different to teaching Maths, English, Science or PE to people with severe or profound learning difficulties. We need to teach in ways that are appropriate to the learning style and ability of the individual.

There are times, however, when even the best laid plans come to nought and it is important that we at least address the possible reasons.

The school or the Local Education Authority is not willing or able to fund the necessary staffing

Dealing effectively with challenging behaviour is not cheap – and I've never claimed that it is. It is often the case that effective programmes can be put into place without recourse to additional staffing, but is also often the case that they cannot – especially in the short term. In fact it is often the case that the behaviour continues because the school or LEA has not put in sufficient resources at an early enough stage. I don't wish to repeat the arguments made in Chapter 1 'What is challenging behaviour?' but the 'halfpenny worth of tar' argument definitely holds true with behaviour. Sorting behavioural challenges out effectively in the early stages (applying a halfpenny worth of tar to the ship's hull) saves the prospect of the school failing, the child becoming uneducable and a residential placement ensuing (saves the hole becoming bigger and bigger until the ship sinks). Those of us who are managers within whatever service we offer – be it school, respite care, out of school clubs or even at home – have a responsibility to argue the case with whoever holds the purse strings. We can make a very sound economic case and we should make every effort to do so.

The child, young person or adult with challenging behaviour is not appropriately placed in the class or school

It is difficult to over-estimate the importance of teaching at a level appropriate for the individual if behavioural challenges are to be kept to a minimum, and those that arise are to be dealt with effectively. The learning styles of people with SLD, PMLD and ASD (never mind about moderate learning difficulties) are radically different from each other. It **may** be reasonable to expect teachers and TAs to have a thorough knowledge of the three (and perhaps four) categories of disability, but it seems wholly unreasonable to expect teachers and TAs to differentiate teaching within the same class across the three (and perhaps four) categories. There are, I'm sure, some staff who can do it, but these will be the exception (and exceptional!) which prove the rule that it is just too difficult to achieve success consistently across such a wide range of need. The increasing trend towards large special schools covering a range of need is one, therefore, that has to be thought about **very** carefully. I understand that this trend may well be a matter of economies of scale, but the economic argument could easily backfire if classes become unmanageable.

Nonetheless, the case for such multi-category schools is still as strong if each of the categories of learning need were taught separately rather than in the same class. Inclusion time could be planned within areas like drama and dance and music as well as mealtimes, playtimes and assemblies. I don't believe that inclusion is about offering the **same** education to all, because the **same** education will not suit everyone, any more than the same size clothes will fit everyone. Inclusion is surely about providing all with an equal opportunity to an education appropriate to their needs. It is surely far more about quality than quantity.

The child is appropriately placed from a learning perspective, but the behaviours are insurmountable

Of course, even if we get it all right, do all the right things, follow the principles steadfastly and are patient and loving and persistent, there is no **absolute** guarantee of success. There are bound to be some learners whose needs are so great that residential care is the only answer. These learners will be those for whom consistency is paramount across every hour of every day and who place the greatest strain upon normal family life. They will be those whose needs stretch the resources of the education, social and health agencies beyond the point of an effective service. It is definitely the case that these instances will be very much the exception, but nonetheless they are bound to occur, however occasionally, and the only answer is probably a residential placement. Certainly these cases will need to have as their priority the best interests of the child, young person or adult, but we cannot ignore the sometimes dangerous degree of strain they can place on parents and siblings.

Lastly in this chapter, there are two areas that I have barely touched upon in the book, that is, the use of drugs to control behaviour and the use of restraint to control behaviour.

Drugs

There is no doubt that drugs which claim to control behaviour have become considerably more sophisticated over the last ten years or so. Some such as Ritalin (and other similar compounds with differing brand names) have almost become commonplace with certain diagnosed conditions like ADHD. There has to be a question mark against the extraordinary rise of diagnosed ADHD and the equivalent extraordinary rise in the prescription of drugs, but that is beyond the scope of this book. Others drugs, such as Resperidone, are lauded as 'cures for autism'! They can possibly be useful but only as a **very last** resort when **all other options** have been tried and have **demonstrably failed**. Understandably, those working in medicine (both GPs and hospital staff) have a tendency to advise in favour of medication, but it is a poor option to take because it does not give the learner the opportunity to take control of their own behaviour. There may be cases where there is a clear psychotic condition as well as a learning difficulty and this is a different matter entirely, but these psychoses will probably only become apparent in the late teens and will require a clinical psychiatric diagnosis.

Restraint

Any school, respite centre, youth centre or after school club which has regular contact with children, young people or adults with challenging behaviour would be very well advised to train their staff in techniques for restraint or, to use the more politically correct terminology, positive handling techniques. There are a number of organisations which undertake training, though the main ones will be recommended by BILD (the British Institute for Learning Disabilities) and can be contacted through them at www.bild.org.uk.

I can only personally speak for Team-Teach, since I am an accredited trainer, and am very happy to recommend them to you. They can be contacted through www.team-teach.co.uk. It is, however, vital that we recognise that any recourse to restraint is an emergency and it should certainly not be used as a replacement for a behaviour management policy. There is no doubt that using restraint techniques on a regular basis is an indication that we have failed in our attempts to teach learners better ways of communicating their needs. There may be exceptional circumstances – especially when dealing with those with emotional, social and behavioural difficulties (ESBD) – but for SLD, PMLD and ASD use of restraint techniques **must** be the occasional exception rather than the norm.

Some final thoughts

I have tried throughout this book to give both a theoretical and a practical background on which to base your work with the children, young people and adults with SLD, PMLD and ASD who are expressing challenging behaviours; but I do not want this work to be seen as either theoretical or academic in nature. This is a book about practice, and it is very much about practice making perfect. There's a very appropriate story about Gary Player, in his time one of the world's very best golfers. After finishing a particularly low-scoring round, one commentator remarked that he thought Player might have ridden his luck that day. 'It's odd isn't it,' replied Player, 'that the more I practise the luckier I get!' And this is largely at the core of the book, because I've made more mistakes than you could shake a stick at but still passionately believe that the next time I'm going to get it right if I keep working at it. I don't actually have all the answers – no-one does – and I think it's important that readers accept that temporary failure, puzzlement and uncertainty are par for the course when dealing with challenging behaviour. The point is that we need to work through these problems rather than give up, but even the best are going to face difficulties on a fairly regular basis.

I have also, in my final summary, tried to pick out one word that might sum up the philosophy espoused in this book, but cannot. All of those seven words are **so** important that I'd have them tattooed in reverse on everyone's forehead, so that when they look in the mirror in the morning thinking about the dreadful day ahead with Tommy, Johnnie, Jascinta or Ahmed there is at least something to base our work upon.

I do, nonetheless, passionately believe that we both can make a difference and do make a difference, and we are, in so many cases, the difference between despair and hope.

And five last words – **the very best of luck!**

References

Books

Ainscow, M. and Tweddle, D. A. (1988), *Preventing Classroom Failure: An Objectives Approach*. London: David Fulton.

Aird, R. (2001), *The Education and Care of Children with Severe, Profound and Multiple Difficulties*. London: David Fulton.

Asperger, H. (1944), 'Die "autistischen Psychopathen" im Kindesalter', *Archiv für Psychiatrie und Nervenkrankheiten*, 117: 76–136.

Ayres, A. J., Erwin, P. and Mailloux, Z. (2004), *Love Jean: Inspiration for Families Living with Dysfunction of Sensory Integration*. California: Crestport Press.

Baird, G., Simonoff, E., Pickles, A., Chandler, S., Loucas, T., Meldrum, D. and Charman, T. (2006), 'Prevalence of disorders of the autism spectrum in a population cohort of children in South Thames: the Special Needs and Autism Project (SNAP)', *The Lancet*, 368 (9531): 210–15.

Barnard, J., Braoch, S., Potter, D. and Prior, A. (2002), *Autism in Schools: Crisis or Challenge?* London: The National Autistic Society.

Baron-Cohen, S., Leslie, A. and Frith, U. (1985), 'Does the autistic child have a "theory of mind"?', *Cognition*, 21: 37–46.

Bates, E., Camaioni, L. and Volterra, V. (1975), 'The acquisition of performatives prior to speech', *Merrill-Palmer Quarterly* 21.

Bogdashina, O. (2006), *Theory of Mind and the Triad of Perspectives on Autism and Asperger Syndrome*. London: Jessica Kingsley.

Brown, C. (1954), *My Left Foot*. London: Secker and Warburg.

Camaioni, L. (1992), 'Mind knowledge in infancy: the emergence of intentional communication', *Early Development and Parenting*, 1(1): 15–22.

Carr, E. G. and Durand, V. M. (1985), 'Reducing behavior problems through functional communication and training', *Journal of Applied Behavior Analysis*, 18(2): 111–26.

Clements, J. and Zarkowska, E. (2000), *Behavioural Concerns and Autistic Spectrum Disorders*. London: Jessica Kingsley.

Collis, M. and Lacey, P. (1996), *Interactive Approaches to Teaching*. London: David Fulton.

Cutler, I. (2000), 'Down the Numeracy Strategy Road', *The SLD Experience*. 26: 7–8.

Dunst, C. (1980), *A Clinical and Educational Manual for Use with the Uzgiris and Hunt Scales of Infant Psychological Development*. Austin, TX: Pro-Ed.

Edelson, M., 'Rett Syndrome', www.autism.org accessed on 7 Nov 2006.

Ehlers, S. and Gillberg, C. (1993), 'The epidemiology of Asperger's Syndrome: a total population study', *Journal of Child Psychology & Psychiatry*, 34(8): 1327–50.

Emerson, E. (1995), *Challenging Behaviour: Analysis and Intervention in People with Learning Disabilities*. Cambridge: Cambridge University Press.

Emerson, E. (2001), *Challenging Behaviour: Analysis and Intervention in People with Severe Intellectual Difficulties*. Cambridge: Cambridge University Press.

Fleisher, M. (2006), *Survival Strategies for People on the Autistic Spectrum*. London: Jessica Kingsley.

Frith, U. (1989), *Autism and Asperger Syndrome*. Cambridge: Cambridge University Press.

Frost, L. and Bondy, A. (2001) *The Picture Exchange Communication System Training Manual*. Newark, NJ: Pyramid Education.

Gibson, L. (1989), *Literacy Learning in the Early Years: Through Children's Eyes*. London: Cassell.

Goldbart, J. (1994), 'Opening the Communication Curriculum to students with PMLDs', in J. Ware, *Educating Children with Profound and Multiple Learning Difficulties*. London: David Fulton.

Grandin, T. (2006), *Thinking in Pictures*. New York: Vintage Press.

Grandin, T. and Scariano, M. (1986), *Emergence: Labelled Autistic*. Novato, CA: Arena.

Gray, C. (2000), *The New Social Story Book*. Arlington, TX: Future Horizons.

Grossman, H. J., Begab, M. J., Cantwell, M. D., Clements, J. D., Eyman, R. K., Meyers, C. E., Tarjan, G. and Waren, S. A. (1983), *Classification in Mental Retardation*. Washington, DC: American Association on Mental Deficiency.

Grove N. (1998), *Reading for All*. London: David Fulton.

Grove, N. (2005), *Ways into Literature: Stories, Plays and Poems for Pupils with SEN*. London: David Fulton.

Haddon, M. (2004), *The Curious Incident of the Dog in the Night-Time*. London: Vintage.

Harris, J. (1995), 'Responding to pupils with SLD, who present challenging behaviour', *British Journal of Special Education*, 22(3): 109–15.

Harris, J., Cook, M. and Upton, G. (1993), 'Challenging behaviour in the classroom', in J. Harris (ed.), *Innovations in Educating Children with Severe Learning Difficulties*. Chorley, Lancs: Lisieux Hall.

Harris, J., Cook, M. and Upton, G. (1996), *Pupils with Severe Learning Disabilities Who Present Challenging Behaviour*. Kidderminster: BILD.

Harris, J., Hewett, D. and Hogg, J. (2001), *Positive Approaches to Challenging Behaviour*. Kidderminster: BILD.

Hewett, D. (ed.) (1998a), *Challenging Behaviour: Principles and Practices*. London: David Fulton.

Hewett, D. (1998b), 'Challenging behaviour is normal', in P. Lacey and C. Ouvry, (1998), *People with Profound and Multiple Learning Difficulties*. London: David Fulton.

HMSO (2003), *Every Child Matters*. London: HMSO.

Hogg, J. and Sebba, J. (1986), *Profound Retardation and Multiple Impairment, Vol. 1 Development and Learning*. Beckenham: Croom Helm.

Imray, P. (2005), 'Moving towards simple, understandable and workable definitions of SLD and PMLD', *The SLD Experience*, 42: 33–7.

Jackson, L. (2002), *Freaks, Geeks and Asperger Syndrome*. London: Jessica Kingsley.

Jones, G. (2002), *Educational Provision for Children with Autism and Asperger Syndrome*. London: David Fulton.

Jordan, R. (2001), *Autism with Severe Learning Difficulties*. London: Souvenir Press.

Kangas, K. and Lloyd, L. (1988). 'Early cognitive skills as prerequisites to augmentative and alternative communication use: What are we waiting for?', *Augmentative and Alternative Communication*, 4: 211–21.

Kanner, L. (1943), 'Autistic disturbances of affective contact', *The Nervous Child*, 2: 217–50.

Kiernan, C. (1985), 'The development of communication and cognition', in J. Dobbing (ed.), *Scientific Studies in Mental Retardation*. Macmillan Press: Royal Society of Medicine.

Kiernan, C., Reid, B. and Goldbart, J. (1987), *Foundations of Communication and Language*. Manchester: Manchester University Press.

Lacey, P. (2006), 'What is inclusive literacy?', *The SLD Experience*, 46: 3–7.

Latham, C. (2005), *Developing and Using a Communication Book*. Oxford: ACE Centre Advisory Trust.

Latham, C. and Miles, A. (2002), *Communication, Curriculum and Classroom Practice*. London: David Fulton.

Lawson, W. (2001), *Understanding and Working with the Spectrum of Autism: An Insider's View*. London: Jessica Kingsley.

Lorenz, S. (1998), *Children with Down's Syndrome*. London: David Fulton.

Luckasson, R., Coulter, D. L., Polloway, E. A., Reiss, S., Schalock, R. L., Snell, M. E., Spitalnik, D. M. and Stark, J. A. (1992), *Mental Retardation: Definition, Classification and Systems of Supports*. Washington, DC: American Association on Mental Deficiency.

Male, D. B. (1996), 'Who goes to SLD schools?', *Journal of Applied Research in Intellectual Disabilities*, 9(4): 307–23.

Male, D. B. (2006), 'Recent research', *The SLD Experience*, 46: 27–39.

McBrien, J. and Felce, D. (1992), *Working with People Who Have Severe Learning Disability and Challenging Behaviour: A Practical Handbook on the Behavioural Approach*. Kidderminster: BILD Publications.

McGee, J. J. and Menolascino, F. J. (1991), *Beyond Gentle Teaching: A Nonaversive Approach to Helping Those in Need*. New York: Plenum Press.

Murphy, G. and Wilson, B. (1985), *Self-Injurious Behaviour*. Kidderminster: BIMH Publications.

New English Dictionary (1994), New Lanark: Geddes and Grosset.

Nind, M. and Hewett, D. (1994), *Access to Communication*. London: David Fulton.

Nind, M. and Hewett, D. (2001), *A Practical Guide to Intensive Interaction*. Kidderminster: BILD.

O'Brien, T. (1998), *Promoting Positive Behaviour*. London: David Fulton.

Ockelford, A. (2002), *Objects of Reference: Promoting Early Symbolic Communication*. London: RNIB.

Ouvrey, C. (1998), 'Making relationships', in P. Lacey and C. Ouvrey (eds) *People with Profound and Multiple Learning Disabilities*. London: David Fulton.

Park, K. (1998), 'Form and function in early communication', *The SLD Experience*, 21: 2–5.

Park, K. (2004), *Interactive Storytelling: Developing Inclusive Stories for Children and Adults*. Bicester: Speechmark.

Peeters, T. (2000), 'The language of objects', in S. Powell, *Helping Children with Autism to Learn*. London: David Fulton.

Piaget, J. (1953), *The Origins of Intelligence in Children*. New York: International Press.

QCA (2001), *Planning, Teaching and Assessing the Curriculum for Pupils with Learning Difficulties*. London: QCA.

Robbins, B. (2000), *Inclusive Mathematics 5–11*. London: Cassell.

Segar, M. (1996), *Coping: A Survival Guide for People with Asperger Syndrome*. Nottingham: Elizabeth Newson Centre: Available on www.autismandcomputing.org.uk, accessed 7 Nov 2006.

Skinner, B. F. (1953), *Science and Human Behaviour*. New York: Macmillan.

Smith Myles, B., Tapscott Cook, K., Miller, N., Rinner, L. and Robbins, L. (2001), *Asperger Syndrome and Sensory Issues: Practical Solutions for Making Sense of the World*. Kansas: Autism Asperger Publishing Company.

Staves, L. (2001), *Mathematics for Children with Severe and Profound Learning Difficulties*. London: David Fulton.

Sturmey, P., Rickets, R. W. and Goza, A. (1993), 'A review of the aversives debate: an American perspective', in S. Jones and C. Eayres (eds), *Challenging Behaviour and Intellectual Disability. A Psychological Perspective*. Kidderminster: BILD.

Uzgiris, I. and Hunt, J. (1975), *Assessment in Infancy: Ordinal Scales of Psychological Development*. Urbana: University of Illinois Press.

Ware, J. (2003), *Creating a Responsive Environment for People with Profound and Multiple Learning Difficulties*. London: David Fulton.

Whitaker, P. (2001), *Challenging Behaviour and Autism: Making Sense – Making Progress*. London: The National Autistic Society.

Williams, D. (1999), *Nobody Nowhere*. London: Jessica Kingsley.

Wing, L. and Gould, J. (1979), 'Severe impairments of social interaction and associated abnormalities in children: epidemiology and classification', *Journal of Autism and Developmental Disorders*, 9: 11–29.

Zarkowska, E. and Clements, J. (1994), *Problem Behaviour and People with Severe Learning Disabilities: The S.T.A.R. Approach*. London: Chapman and Hall.

Websites

www.learningandteaching.info/learning/behaviour for information on behaviourism.

www.bild.org.uk for BILD (the British Institute for Learning Disabilities) and recommended organisations to train staff in positive handling (restraint) techniques.

www.nas.org.uk for information on autism from the National Autistic Society.

www.pdacontact.org.uk. for information on Pathological Demand Avoidance (PDA).

www.team-teach.co.uk. for training staff in positive handling (restraint) techniques.

Index